To

Olivia B.

From

Coach Cremen

Date

Christmas '05

Values
for Life

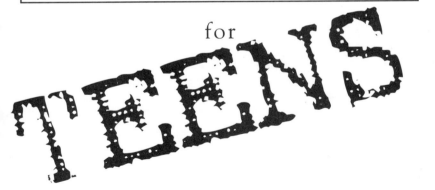

for
TEENS

The quoted ideas expressed in this book (but not scripture verses) are not, in all cases, exact quotations, as some have been edited for clarity and brevity. In all cases, the author has attempted to maintain the speaker's original intent. In some cases, quoted material for this book was obtained from secondary sources, primarily print media. While every effort was made to ensure the accuracy of these sources, the accuracy cannot be guaranteed. For additions, deletions, corrections or clarifications in future editions of this text, please write FAMILY CHRISTIAN PRESS.

Scripture quotations are taken from:

The Holy Bible, King James Version

The Holy Bible, New International Version (NIV) Copyright © 1973, 1978, 1984, by International Bible Society. Used by permission of Zondervan Publishing House. All rights reserved.

The New American Standard Bible®, (NASB) Copyright © 1960, 1962, 1963, 1968, 1971, 1972, 1973, 1975, 1977, 1995 by The Lockman Foundation. Used by permission.

The Holy Bible, New King James Version (NKJV) Copyright © 1982 by Thomas Nelson, Inc. Used by permission.

The Holy Bible, New Living Translation, (NLT) Copyright © 1996. Used by permission of Tyndale House Publishers, Inc., Wheaton, Illinois 60189. All rights reserved.

New Century Version®. (NCV) Copyright © 1987, 1988, 1991 by Word Publishing, a division of Thomas Nelson, Inc. All rights reserved. Used by permission.

The Holy Bible: Revised Standard Version (RSV). Copyright 1946, 1952, 1959, 1973 by the Division of Christian Education of the National Council of the Churches of Christ in the United States of America. All rights reserved. Used by permission.

The Holy Bible, The Living Bible (TLB), Copyright © 1971 owned by assignment by Illinois Regional Bank N.A. (as trustee). Used by permission of Tyndale House Publishers, Inc., Wheaton, Illinois 60189. All rights reserved.

The Message (MSG) This edition issued by contractual arrangement with NavPress, a division of The Navigators, U.S.A. Originally published by NavPress in English as THE MESSAGE: The Bible in Contemporary Language copyright 2002-2003 by Eugene Peterson. All rights reserved.

The Holman Christian Standard Bible™ (HCSB) Copyright © 1999, 2000, 2001 by Holman Bible Publishers. Used by permission.

Cover Design by Kim Russell / Wahoo Designs
Page Layout by Bart Dawson

ISBN 1-58334-286-9

Printed in the United States of America

Values
for Life

for

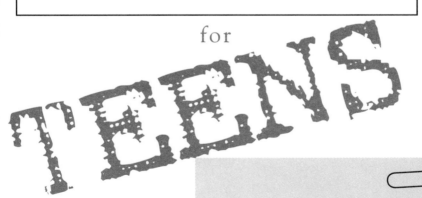

Unchanging Wisdom
for a Godly Life

In all your ways acknowledge Him, and He shall direct your paths.

Proverbs 3:6 NKJV

Table of Contents

Introduction   12

1.   Values for Life • Values   14
2.   Why Worship? • Worship   18
3.   Wisdom According to Whom? • Wisdom   22
4.   Beyond Worry • Worry   26
5.   The Value of Hard Work • Work   30
6.   The Power of Purpose • Purpose   34
7.   Walking in Truth • Truth   38
8.   A New Creation • Transformation   42
9.   A Humble Heart • Humility   46
10. Time: The Fabric of Life • Time   50
11. Directing Our Thoughts • Thoughts   54
12. Materialism 101: The Value of Stuff • Materialism   58
13. The Wisdom of Thanksgiving • Thanksgiving   62
14. A Compelling Testimony: Yours • Testimony   66
15. The Value of Your Daily Devotional • Devotional   70
16. A Lifetime of Spiritual Growth • Spiritual Growth   74
17. Speaking with a Voice of Triumph • Self-esteem   78
18. Character-building 101 • Character   82
19. Making All Things New • Renewal   86
20. Too Many Questions? • Questions   90
21. The Right Thing to Do • Behavior   94
22. Putting Off Till Tomorrow • Procrastination   98
23. Putting Possessions in Proper Perspective • Possessions   102

24. The Power of the Words We Speak • Speech   106

25. The Size of Your Problems • Perspective   110

26. God Is Perfect; We Are Not • Perfectionism   114

27. Trusting His Timetable • God's Timing   118

28. Discovering His Peace • Peace   122

29. Faith-filled Christian • Optimism   126

30. Behaviors That Are Pleasing to Whom? • Peer Pressure   130

31. Opportunities Everywhere • Opportunities   134

32. An Obedient Heart • Obedience   138

33. Really Living Means Really Loving • Love   142

34. The Courage to Dream • Dreams   146

35. Beyond Loneliness • Loneliness   150

36. Life with a Capital L • Life   154

37. Valuing God's Guidance • God's Guidance   158

38. The Choice to Rejoice • Joy   162

39. Hope Now! • Hope   166

40. Valuing God's Word • The Bible   170

41. Good Samaritan 101 • Helping Others   174

42. The Temple of God That Belongs to You • Fitness   178

43. The Rule That Is Golden • Golden Rule   182

44. The Power of Simplicity • Simplicity   186

45. God's Surprising Plans • God's Plans   190

46. He Is Here • God's Presence   194

47. A Willingness to Serve • Service   198

48. Trusting God's Love • God's Love   202

49. God's Gift of Grace • God's Grace   206

50. On Beyond Failure • Disappointment and Failure   210

51. The Cheerful Giver • Giving   216

52. Forgiving and Forgetting • Forgiveness   220

53. Following Christ • Following Christ   224

54. A Lifetime of Learning • Knowledge   228

55. Strength from Family • Family   232

56. A Foundation of Faith • Faith   236

57. Possibilities According to God • God's Power   240

58. The Power of Encouragement • Encouragement   244

59. During Those Difficult Days • Difficult Days   248

60. Above and Beyond Anger • Anger   252

61. The Dating Game • Dating   256

62. Living Courageously • Courage   260

63. Valuing Your Gifts • Talents   264

64. Claiming Contentment in a Discontented World • Contentment   268

65. Trusting the Quiet Voice • Conscience   272

66. The Power of Patience • Patience   276

67. Comforting Those in Need • Comforting Others   280

68. Becoming a Great Communicator • Communication   284

69. The Joys of Friendship • Friends   288

70. Cheerful Christianity • Cheerfulness   292

71. Living above the Daily Whine • Attitude   296

72. The Righteous Life • Righteousness   300

73. Tackling Tough Times • Adversity   304

74. Acceptance for Today • Acceptance   308

75. This Is the Day . . . • Today   312

Index of Topics   316

Introduction

O kay, here's a question: How many decisions do you make in a typical day? When you stop to think about it, you make hundreds of choices each day, usually without too much forethought. Of course, most of these choices are relatively small ones, like what to do at a given moment or what to say or how to direct your thoughts. Occasionally, you will face major decisions, like choosing to be a Christian or choosing a profession or choosing a mate. But whatever choices you face, whether they're big, little, or somewhere in between, you can be sure of this: the quality of your choices will make an enormous difference in the quality of your life.

Your choices are shaped by your values. Simply put, your values determine, to a surprising extent, the quality of the decisions you make and the direction that your life will take. And that's why the ideas in this book are so important.

This book addresses Christian values that can—and should—shape your life. You may find it helpful to read the book from cover to cover, or you may decide to scan the Table of Contents and then turn to chapters that seem particularly important to you. Either way, the ideas on these pages will serve to remind you of God's commandments, God's promises, God's love, and God's Son—all things that are crucially important as you establish priorities for the coming day *and* for all the days that follow it.

Whatever you do, do all to the glory of God.

1 Corinthians 10:31 NKJV

Values for Life

You will show me the path of life; in Your presence is fullness of joy;
at Your right hand are pleasures forevermore.

Psalm 16:11 NKJV

Every day, society tries to shape your values. Society wants you to focus on the distractions and temptations of our troubled, 21st-century world. But society's value system is far different from God's value system. And if you're wise, you'll pay more attention to God and less attention to the things that distance you from God.

When God's values become your values, then you share in His abundance and His peace. But, if you place the world's priorities in front of God's priorities, you're asking for trouble . . . BIG trouble.

You live in a world that is filled with countless opportunities to make big-time mistakes. The world seems to cry, "Worship me with your time, your money, your energy, and your thoughts!" But God commands otherwise: He commands you to worship Him and Him alone; everything else must be secondary.

Do you want to experience God's peace and His blessings? If so, then you must build your life upon a value system that puts God first. So, when you're faced with a difficult choice or a powerful temptation, seek God's counsel and trust the counsel that He gives. Invite God into your heart and live according to His commandments. Study His Word and talk to Him often. When you do, you will share in the abundance and peace that only God can give.

Once you have thoroughly examined your values and articulated them, you will be able to steer your life by them.

John Maxwell

Values for Life

Whose values? You can have the values that the world holds dear, or you can have the values that God holds dear, but you can't have both. The decision is yours . . . and so are the consequences.

Timeless Wisdom for Godly Living

You cannot be the person God meant you to be, and you cannot live the life he meant you to live, unless you live from the heart.

John Eldredge

Holiness is not an impossibility for any of us.

Elisabeth Elliot

God's Way is not a matter of mere talk;
it's an empowered life.
1 Corinthians 4:20 MSG

He doesn't need an abundance of words. He doesn't need a dissertation about your life. He just wants your attention. He wants your heart.

Kathy Troccoli

By choosing to embrace and practice good values every day, you may not always get what you desire, but you will always be the person you desire to be.

John Maxwell

More Words from God's Word

Walk in a manner worthy of the God who calls you into His own kingdom and glory.

1 Thessalonians 2:12 NASB

Therefore, since we have this ministry, as we have received mercy, we do not give up. Instead, we have renounced shameful secret things, not walking in deceit or distorting God's message, but in God's sight we commend ourselves to every person's conscience by an open display of the truth.

2 Corinthians 4:1-2 HCSB

We must not become tired of doing good. We will receive our harvest of eternal life at the right time if we do not give up.

Galatians 6:9 NCV

My Values for Life

I will focus my thoughts and energies on living a principled life.

I will study God's Word and do my best to live according to God's commandments.

I will seek to share my value system with family and friends.

Check Your Value		
High	Med.	Low
—	—	—
—	—	—
—	—	—

Why Worship?

Shout with joy to the LORD, O earth!
Worship the LORD with gladness. Come before him, singing with joy.

Psalm 100:1-2 NLT

Why do you attend church? Is it because of your sincere desire to worship and to praise God? Hopefully so. Yet far too many Christians attend worship services because they believe they are "supposed to go to church" or because they feel "pressured" to attend. Still others go to church for "social" reasons. But make no mistake: the best reason to attend church is out of a sincere desire to please God, to praise God, to experience God, and to discern God's will for your life.

Some people may tell you that they don't engage in worship. Don't believe them. All of mankind is engaged in worship. The question is not whether we worship, but what we worship. Wise men and women choose to worship God. When they do, they are blessed with a plentiful harvest of joy, peace, and abundance. Other people choose to distance themselves from God by foolishly worshiping things that are intended to bring personal gratification but not spiritual gratification. Such choices often have tragic consequences.

If we place our love for material possessions or social status above our love for God—or if we yield to the countless temptations of this world—we find ourselves engaged in a struggle between good and evil, a clash between God and Satan. Our responses to these struggles have implications that echo throughout our families and throughout our communities.

How can we ensure that we cast our lot with God? We do so, in part, by the practice of regular, purposeful worship in the company of fellow believers. When we worship God faithfully and fervently, we are blessed. When we fail to worship God, for whatever reason, we forfeit the spiritual gifts that might otherwise be ours.

We must worship our Heavenly Father, not just with our words, but also with deeds. We must honor Him, praise Him, and obey Him. As we seek to find purpose and meaning for our lives, we must first seek His purpose and His will. For believers, God comes first. Always first.

Authentic worship flows out of telling the truth, out of facing our greatest fears, out of finding peace in unexpected places.

Sheila Walsh

Values for Life

The best way to worship God . . . is to worship Him sincerely and often.

Timeless Wisdom for Godly Living

Worship and worry cannot live in the same heart; they are mutually exclusive.

Ruth Bell Graham

When God is at the center of your life, you worship. When he's not, you worry.

Rick Warren

God is spirit, and those who worship him must worship in spirit and truth.
John 4:24 NCV

It's the definition of worship: A hungry heart finding the Father's feast. A searching soul finding the Father's face. A wandering pilgrim spotting the Father's house. Finding God. Finding God seeking us. This is worship. This is a worshiper.

Max Lucado

You were Lord of the heavens before time was time, and Lord of all lords You will be! We bow down and we worship You, Lord.

Twila Paris

More Words from God's Word

For it is written, "You shall worship the Lord your God, and Him only you shall serve."

Matthew 4:10 NKJV

And every day they devoted themselves to meeting together in the temple complex, and broke bread from house to house. They ate their food with gladness and simplicity of heart, praising God and having favor with all the people. And every day the Lord added those being saved to them.

Acts 2:46-47 HCSB

If anyone is thirsty, he should come to Me and drink!

John 7:37 HCSB

I was glad when they said to me, "Let us go to the house of the Lord."

Psalm 122:1 NLT

My Values for Life

	Check Your Value		
	High	Med.	Low
I consider each day an opportunity to praise God and to worship Him.	—	—	—
I understand the importance of being actively involved in my church.	—	—	—
I consider praise and worship to be a regular part of my day.	—	—	—
I sincerely want to worship God in spirit and truth.	—	—	—

Worship

Wisdom According to Whom?

But the wisdom that is from above is first pure, then peaceable,
gentle, willing to yield, full of mercy and good fruits,
without partiality and without hypocrisy.

James 3:17 NKJV

Are you a wise guy (or girl)? And, are you becoming a little wiser every day? Hopefully so. All of us would like to be wise, but not all of us are willing to do the work that is required to become wise. Why? Because wisdom isn't free—it takes time and effort to acquire.

To become wise, we must seek God's wisdom and live according to His Word. To become wise, we must seek wisdom with consistency and purpose. To become wise, we must not only learn the lessons of the Christian life, but we must also live by them.

If you sincerely desire to become wise—and if you seek to share your hard-earned wisdom with others—your actions must give credence to your words. The best way to share one's wisdom— perhaps the only way—is not by words, but by example.

Wisdom is like a savings account: If you add to it consistently, then eventually you'll have a great sum. The secret to success is consistency. Do you seek wisdom? Then seek it every day, and seek it in the right place. That place, of course, is, first and foremost, the Word of God.

Wise people listen to wise instruction,
especially instruction from the Word of God.

Warren Wiersbe

How much better to get wisdom than gold,
to choose understanding rather than silver!

Proverbs 16:16 NIV

Values for Life

Need wisdom? God's got it. If you want it, then study God's Word and associate with godly people.

Timeless Wisdom for Godly Living

Having a doctrine pass before the mind is not what the Bible means by knowing the truth. It's only when it reaches down deep into the heart that the truth begins to set us free, just as a key must penetrate a lock to turn it, or as rainfall must saturate the earth down to the roots in order for your garden to grow.

John Eldredge

The fruit of wisdom is Christlikeness, peace, humility, and love. And, the root of it is faith in Christ as the manifested wisdom of God.

J. I. Packer

Those who are wise will shine like the brightness of the heavens, and those who lead many to righteousness, like the stars for ever and ever.
Daniel 12:3 NIV

Wisdom is the God-given ability to see life with rare objectivity and to handle life with rare stability.

Charles Swindoll

Wisdom is knowledge applied. Head knowledge is useless on the battlefield. Knowledge stamped on the heart makes one wise.

Beth Moore

More Words from God's Word

Wisdom

Every morning he wakes me. He teaches me to listen like a student. The Lord God helps me learn . . . .

Isaiah 50:4-5 NCV

Let the word of Christ dwell in you richly in all wisdom; teaching and admonishing one another in psalms and hymns and spiritual songs, singing with grace in your hearts to the Lord.

Colossians 3:16 KJV

But also for this very reason, giving all diligence, add to your faith virtue, to virtue knowledge.

2 Peter 1:5 NKJV

Therefore everyone who hears these words of mine and puts them into practice is like a wise man who built his house on the rock.

Matthew 7:24 NIV

My Values for Life

I will continually remind myself of God's wisdom by reading the Bible each day.

I do my best to live wisely by obeying God's rules.

I try to select friends who can help me become a better and wiser person.

Check Your Value		
High	Med.	Low
—	—	—
—	—	—
—	—	—

Beyond Worry

I was very worried, but you comforted me . . . .

Psalm 94:19 NCV

Because you have the ability to think, you also have the ability to worry. Even if you're a very faithful Christian, you may be plagued by occasional periods of discouragement and doubt. Even though you trust God's promise of salvation—even though you sincerely believe in God's love and protection—you may find yourself upset by the countless details of everyday life. Jesus understood your concerns when He spoke the reassuring words found in the 6th chapter of Matthew.

Therefore I say to you, do not worry about your life, what you will eat or what you will drink; nor about your body, what you will put on. Is not life more than food and the body more than clothing? Look at the birds of the air, for they neither sow nor reap nor gather into barns; yet your heavenly Father feeds them. Are you not of more value than they? Which of you by worrying can add one cubit to his stature? . . . Therefore do not worry about tomorrow, for tomorrow will worry about its own things. Sufficient for the day is its own trouble. vv. 25-27, 34 NKJV

Where is the best place to take your worries? Take them to God. Take your troubles to Him; take your fears to Him; take your doubts to Him; take your weaknesses to Him; take your sorrows to Him . . . and leave them all there. Seek protection from the One who offers you eternal salvation; build your spiritual house upon the

Rock that cannot be moved.

Perhaps you are concerned about your future or your relationships. Or perhaps you are simply a "worrier" by nature. If so, choose to make Matthew 6 a regular part of your daily Bible reading. This beautiful passage will remind you that God still sits in His heaven and you are His beloved child. Then, perhaps, you will worry a little less and trust God a little more, and that's as it should be because God is trustworthy . . . and you are protected.

Worry does not empty tomorrow of its sorrow; it empties today of its strength.

Corrie ten Boom

Values for Life

Remember: This, too, will pass: And remember that it will pass more quickly if you spend more time solving problems and less time fretting over them.

Timeless Wisdom for Godly Living

The busier we are, the easier it is to worry, the greater the temptation to worry, the greater the need to be alone with God.

Charles Stanley

Worry is the senseless process of cluttering up tomorrow's opportunities with leftover problems from today.

Barbara Johnson

Our fears for today, our worries about tomorrow, and even the powers of hell can't keep God's love away.

Bill Bright

Give your worries to the Lord, and he will take care of you. He will never let good people down.
Psalm 55:22 NCV

If the glories of heaven were more real to us, if we lived less for material things and more for things eternal and spiritual, we would be less easily disturbed in this present life.

Billy Graham

Walk by faith! Stop the plague of worry. Relax! Learn to say, "Lord, this is Your battle."

Charles Swindoll

More Words from God's Word

Don't fret or worry, Instead of worrying, pray. Let petitions and praises shape your worries into prayers, letting God know your concerns. Before you know it, a sense of God's wholeness, everything coming together for good, will come and settle you down. It's wonderful what happens when Christ displaces worry at the center of your life.

Philippians 4:6-7 MSG

Worry is a heavy load, but a kind word cheers you up.

Proverbs 12:25 NCV

Come to me, all you who are weary and burdened, and I will give you rest. Take my yoke upon you and learn from me, for I am gentle and humble in heart, and you will find rest for your souls. For my yoke is easy and my burden is light.

Matthew 11:28-30 NIV

My Values for Life

I find that the more I am able to trust God, the less worry I experience.

I believe that it is important to try to live in "day-tight" compartments by not fretting too much about yesterday or tomorrow.

When I am worried, I try to think of things that I can do to help solve the things that trouble me.

Check Your Value		
High	Med.	Low
—	—	—
—	—	—
—	—	—

Worry

The Value of Hard Work

Never be lazy in your work, but serve the Lord enthusiastically.

Romans 12:11 NLT

Have you acquired the habit of doing first things first, or are you one of those people who put off important work until the last minute? The answer to this simple question will help determine how well you do your work and how much fun you have doing it.

God's Word teaches the value of hard work. In his second letter to the Thessalonians, Paul warns, " . . . if any would not work, neither should he eat" (3:10 KJV). And the Book of Proverbs proclaims, "One who is slack in his work is brother to one who destroys" (18:9 NIV). In short, God has created a world in which diligence is rewarded and laziness is not. So, whatever it is that you choose to do, do it with commitment, excitement, and vigor. And remember this: Hard work is not simply a proven way to get ahead; it's also part of God's plan for you.

Norman Vincent Peale said, "Think enthusiastically about everything, especially your work." If you're wise, you'll take that advice. When you do, you'll soon discover that the old saying is true: attitude determines altitude.

You have countless opportunities to accomplish great things

for your God, for your family, and for yourself—but you should not expect the work to be easy. So pray as if everything depended upon God, but work as if everything depended upon you. When you do, you should expect very big payoffs. Why? Because when you and God become partners in your work, amazing things are bound to happen.

> How do I love God? By doing beautifully the work I have been given to do, by doing simply that which God entrusted to me, in whatever form it may take.
>
> *Mother Teresa*

Values for Life

Goofing Off Is Contagious. That's why it's important for you to hang out with people who are interested in getting the job done right—and getting it done right now!

Timeless Wisdom for Godly Living

There is no work better than another to please God; to pour water, to wash dishes, to be a cobbler, or an apostle: all is one.

William Tyndale

You will always have joy in the evening if you spend the day fruitfully.

Thomas à Kempis

Help yourself and God will help you.

St. Joan of Arc

And let the loveliness of our Lord, our God, rest on us, confirming the work that we do.

Psalm 90:17 MSG

Dear Lord, let us pray for our daily bread, but let us not be afraid to hunt for our corn-pone with sweat running down the hoe handle.

Sam Jones

I long to accomplish a great and noble task, but it is my chief duty to accomplish small tasks as if they were great and noble.

Helen Keller

More Words from God's Word

But one thing I do: Forgetting what is behind and straining toward what is ahead, I press on toward the goal to win the prize for which God has called me heavenward in Christ Jesus.

Philippians 3:13-14 NIV

Then he said to his disciples, "The harvest is plentiful but the workers are few. Ask the Lord of the harvest, therefore, to send out workers into his harvest field."

Matthew 9:37 NIV

But each person should examine his own work, and then he will have a reason for boasting in himself alone, and not in respect to someone else. For each person will have to carry his own load.

Galatians 6:4-5 HCSB

My Values for Life

I believe that my work is important and that it deserves my best effort.

I believe that the way that I accomplish my job serves as an important example to others.

I believe that I am working, not just for myself, but also for God.

Check Your Value		
High	Med.	Low
—	—	—
—	—	—
—	—	—

The Power of Purpose

*You will show me the path of life; in Your presence is fullness of joy;
at Your right hand are pleasures forevermore.*

Psalm 16:11 NKJV

Life is best lived on purpose, not by accident: the sooner we discover what God intends for us to do with our lives, the better. But God's purposes aren't always clear to us. Sometimes we wander aimlessly in a wilderness of our own making. And sometimes, we struggle mightily against God in a vain effort to find success and happiness through our own means, not His.

Whenever we struggle against God's plans, we suffer. When we resist God's calling, our efforts bear little fruit. Our best strategy, therefore, is to seek God's wisdom and to follow Him wherever He chooses to lead. When we do so, we are blessed.

When we align ourselves with God's purposes, we avail ourselves of His power and His peace. But how can we know precisely what God's intentions are? The answer, of course, is that even the most well-intentioned believers face periods of uncertainty and doubt about the direction of their lives. So, too, will you.

When you arrive at one of life's inevitable crossroads, that is precisely the moment when you should turn your thoughts and prayers toward God. When you do, He will make Himself known to you in a time and manner of His choosing.

Are you earnestly seeking to discern God's purpose for your life? If so, remember this:

1. God has a plan for your life;
2. If you seek that plan sincerely and prayerfully, you will find it;
3. When you discover God's purpose for your life, you will experience abundance, peace, joy, and power—God's power. And that's the only kind of power that really matters.

His life is our light—our purpose
and meaning and reason for living.

Anne Graham Lotz

Values for Life

Discovering God's purpose for your life requires a willingness to be open. God's plan is unfolding day by day. If you keep your eyes and your heart open, He'll reveal His plans. God has big things in store for you, but He may have quite a few lessons to teach you before you are fully prepared to do His will and fulfill His purposes.

Timeless Wisdom for Godly Living

It's incredible to realize that what we do each day has meaning in the big picture of God's plan.

Bill Hybels

We aren't just thrown on this earth like dice tossed across a table. We are lovingly placed here for a purpose.

Charles Swindoll

The promise of the Psalm 121 is not that we shall never stub our toes, but that no injury, no illness, no accident, no distress will have evil power over us, that is, will be able to separate us from God's purposes in us.

Eugene Peterson

The Christian life is not simply following principles but being empowered to fulfill our purpose: knowing and exalting Christ.

Franklin Graham

We are most vulnerable to the piercing winds of doubt when we distance ourselves from the mission and fellowship to which Christ has called us.

Joni Eareckson Tada

To everything there is a season,
a time for every purpose under heaven.
Ecclesiastes 3:1 NKJV

More Words from God's Word

God chose you to be his people, so I urge you now to live the life to which God called you.

Ephesians 4:1 NCV

There is one thing I always do. Forgetting the past and straining toward what is ahead, I keep trying to reach the goal and get the prize for which God called me . . . .

Philippians 3:13-14 NCV

May He grant you according to your heart's desire, and fulfill all your purpose.

Psalm 20:4 NKJV

We know that all things work together for the good of those who love God: those who are called according to His purpose.

Romans 8:28 HCSB

My Values for Life

I understand the importance of discovering God's unfolding purpose for my life.

I consult God on matters great and small.

I remain open to the opportunities and challenges that God places before me.

Check Your Value		
High	Med.	Low
—	—	—
—	—	—
—	—	—

Walking in Truth

*Go after a life of love as if your life depended on it—
because it does. Give yourselves to the gifts God gives you.
Most of all, try to proclaim his truth.*

1 Corinthians 14:1 MSG

Hey, would you like a time-tested, ironclad formula for success? Here it is: guard your integrity like you guard your wallet. It has been said on many occasions and in many ways that honesty is the best policy. For Christians, it is far more important to note that honesty is God's policy. And if we are to be servants worthy of our Savior, Jesus Christ, we must be honest, forthright, and trustworthy.

Telling the truth means telling the whole truth. And that means summoning the courage to deliver bad news when necessary. And for some of us, especially those of us who are card-carrying people pleasers, telling the whole truth can be difficult indeed (especially if we're pretty sure that the truth will make somebody mad). Still, if we wish to fashion successful lives, we've got to learn to be totally truthful—part-time truth-telling doesn't cut the mustard.

Sometimes, honesty is difficult; sometimes, honesty is painful; sometimes, honesty is inconvenient; but honesty is always God's way. In the Book of Proverbs, we read, "The Lord detests lying lips, but he delights in men who are truthful" (12:22 NIV). Clearly, truth is God's way, and it must be our way, too, even when telling the truth is difficult.

Truth will triumph.
The father of truth will win,
and the followers of truth will be saved.

Max Lucado

The best evidence of our having the truth is
our walking in the truth.

Matthew Henry

Values for Life

Knowing the Truth . . . and Living It: Warren Wiersbe writes, "Learning God's truth and getting it into our heads is one thing, but living God's truth and getting it into our characters is quite something else." So don't be satisfied to sit on the sidelines and observe the truth at a distance—live it.

Timeless Wisdom for Godly Living

Having a doctrine pass before the mind is not what the Bible means by knowing the truth. It's only when it reaches down deep into the heart that the truth begins to set us free, just as a key must penetrate a lock to turn it, or as rainfall must saturate the earth down to the roots in order for your garden to grow.

John Eldredge

A person who does not have the Spirit does not accept the truths that come from the Spirit of God. That person thinks they are foolish and cannot understand them, because they can only be judged to be true by the Spirit. The spiritual person is able to judge all things, but no one can judge him.

1 Corinthians 2:14-15 NCV

God will see to it that we understand as much truth as we are willing to obey.

Elisabeth Elliot

For Christians, God himself is the only absolute; truth and ethics are rooted in his character.

Chuck Colson

More Words from God's Word

Be diligent to present yourself approved to God, a worker who doesn't need to be ashamed, correctly teaching the word of truth.

2 Timothy 2:15 HCSB

I have no greater joy than this, to hear of my children walking in the truth.

3 John 1:4 NASB

God also bound himself with an oath, so that those who received the promise could be perfectly sure that he would never change his mind. So God has given us both his promise and his oath. These two things are unchangeable because it is impossible for God to lie. Therefore, we who have fled to him for refuge can take new courage, for we can hold on to his promise with confidence.

Hebrews 6:17-18 NLT

My Values for Life

I believe even when telling the truth is hard, it's always the right thing to do.

I believe unless I build my relationships on honesty, I'm building on a slippery, sandy slope.

I believe that little white lies become king-sized ones. Little white lies have a tendency to grow into big trouble . . . in a hurry.

Check Your Value		
High	Med.	Low
—	—	—
—	—	—
—	—	—

A New Creation

Your old life is dead. Your new life, which is your real life—
even though invisible to spectators—is with Christ in God. He is your life.

Colossians 3:3 MSG

I f you're a Christian, here's a question you should ask yourself:
Are you a different person because of your decision to form
a personal relationship with Jesus? And while you're at it,
here's another question: Does your relationship with Christ make
a meaningful difference in the way that you live your life, or are
you more or less the same person you might be if you were not a
Christian? The answers to these questions will determine the level of
your commitment to God and the direction of your life.

If you're still doing all the same things that non-believers do,
it's time to take an honest look at the current condition of your
faith. Why? Because Jesus doesn't want you to be a run-of-the-mill,
follow-the-crowd kind of person. Jesus intends that you become a
"new creation" through Him. And that's exactly what you should
want for yourself, too.

Each new day presents countless opportunities to put God in
first place, second place, or last place. Oswald Chambers noted,
"If the Spirit of God has transformed you within, you will exhibit
Divine characteristics in your life, not good human characteristics.
God's life in us expresses itself as God's life, not as a human life
trying to be godly."

When you invited Christ to reign over your heart, you became a radically new creation. This day offers yet another chance to behave yourself like that new person. When you do, God will guide your steps and bless your endeavors.

So today, take every step of your journey with God as your traveling companion. Read His Word and follow His commandments. Support only those activities that further God's kingdom and your own spiritual growth. Be an example of the genuine difference that God can make in the lives of people (like you) who follow His will and obey His Word.

In the midst of the pressure and the heat,
I am confident His hand is on my life,
developing my faith until I display His glory,
transforming me into a vessel of honor
that pleases Him!

Anne Graham Lotz

Values for Life

I will invite Jesus into my heart, and I will allow Him to make a difference in my heart.

Timeless Wisdom for Godly Living

If God can fashion the mountains, if God can keep the sun in its orbit, if God can split a sea and dry the ground beneath it so an entire nation can cross, do you doubt that he can transform your character?

Bill Hybels

God's work is not in buildings, but in transformed lives.

Ruth Bell Graham

His message was simple and austere, like his desert surroundings: "Change your life. God's kingdom is here."
Matthew 3:2 MSG

God became man to turn creatures into sons: not simply to produce better men of the old kind but to produce a new kind of man.

C. S. Lewis

Believe and do what God says. The life-changing consequences will be limitless, and the results will be confidence and peace of mind.

Franklin Graham

Once grace has scrubbed the soul, anyone can take their place in the lineage of the Son of God.

Calvin Miller

More Words from God's Word

Now we look inside, and what we see is that anyone united with the Messiah gets a fresh start, is created new. The old life is gone; a new life burgeons! Look at it!

2 Corinthians 5:17 MSG

Don't copy the behavior and customs of this world, but let God transform you into a new person by changing the way you think. Then you will know what God wants you to do, and you will know how good and pleasing and perfect his will really is.

Romans 12:2 NLT

When we were baptized, we were buried with Christ and shared his death. So, just as Christ was raised from the dead by the wonderful power of the Father, we also can live a new life.

Romans 6:4 NCV

My Values for Life

I understand the importance of working to overcome the internal or external obstacles that keep me from becoming the person God wants me to be.

I will ask God to give me the strength, the courage, and the wisdom to free myself from the chains that hold me back.

I will be willing to make major changes in my life if I believe that those changes will make me a better person.

Check Your Value		
High	Med.	Low
—	—	—
—	—	—
—	—	—

A Humble Heart

Do nothing out of rivalry or conceit, but in humility consider others as more important than yourselves.

Philippians 2:3 HCSB

We have heard the phrases on countless occasions: "He's a self-made man," or "she's a self-made woman." In truth, none of us are self-made. We all owe countless debts that we can never repay.

Our first debt, of course, is to our Father in heaven—who has given us everything—and to His Son who sacrificed His own life so that we might live eternally. We are also indebted to ancestors, parents, teachers, friends, spouses, family members, coworkers, fellow believers . . . and the list, of course, goes on.

As Christians, we have a profound reason to be humble: We have been refashioned and saved by Jesus Christ, and that salvation came not because of our own good works but because of God's grace. Thus, we are not "self-made"; we are "God-made" and "Christ-saved." How, then, can we be boastful? The answer, of course, is that, if we are honest with ourselves and with our God, we simply can't be boastful . . . we must, instead, be eternally grateful and exceedingly humble.

Humility is not, in most cases, a naturally-occurring human trait. Most of us, it seems, are more than willing to stick out our chests and say, "Look at me; I did that!" But in our better moments, in the quiet moments when we search the depths of our own hearts, we know better. Whatever "it" is, God did that, not us.

St. Augustine observed, "If you plan to build a tall house of virtues, you must first lay deep foundations of humility." Are you a believer who genuinely seeks to build your house of virtues on a strong foundation of humility? If so, you are wise and you are blessed. But if you've been laboring under the misconception that you're a "self-made" man or woman, it's time to face facts: your blessings come from God. And He deserves the credit.

We can never have more of true faith
than we have of true humility.

Andrew Murray

Values for Life

Do you value humility above status? If so, God will smile upon your endeavors. But if you value status above humility, you're inviting God's displeasure. In short, humility pleases God; pride does not.

Timeless Wisdom for Godly Living

We are never stronger than the moment we admit we are weak.

Beth Moore

Jesus had a humble heart. If He abides in us, pride will never dominate our lives.

Billy Graham

Humility is a thing which must be genuine; the imitation of it is the nearest thing in the world to pride.

C. H. Spurgeon

> *God is against the proud,*
> *but he gives grace to the humble.*
> 1 Peter 5:5 NCV

God is attracted to weakness. He can't resist those who humbly and honestly admit how desperately they need him.

Jim Cymbala

Nothing sets a person so much out of the devil's reach as humility.

Jonathan Edwards

More Words from God's Word

If My people who are called by My name will humble themselves, and pray and seek My face, and turn from their wicked ways, then I will hear from heaven, and will forgive their sin and heal their land.

2 Chronicles 7:14 NKJV

Always be humble, gentle, and patient, accepting each other in love.

Ephesians 4:2 NCV

Humble yourselves in the sight of the Lord, and he shall lift you up.

James 4:10 KJV

He has showed you, O man, what is good. And what does the LORD require of you? To act justly and to love mercy and to walk humbly with your God.

Micah 6:8 NIV

My Values for Life

I place a high priority on the need to remain humble before God.

I understand the importance of remaining humble in my dealings with others.

I genuinely seek to give God the honor that He deserves.

Check Your Value		
High	Med.	Low
—	—	—
—	—	—
—	—	—

Time:
The Fabric of Life

We can't afford to waste a minute, must not squander these precious daylight hours in frivolity and indulgence, in sleeping around and dissipation, in bickering and grabbing everything in sight. Get out of bed and get dressed! Don't loiter and linger, waiting until the very last minute. Dress yourselves in Christ, and be up and about!

Romans 13:13-14 MSG

Do you place a high value on your time? Hopefully you do. After all, time is a precious, nonrenewable gift from God. But sometimes, amid the complications of life here in the 21st-century, you will be sorely tempted to squander the time that God has given you. Why? Because you live in a society filled to the brim with powerful temptations and countless distractions, all of which take time.

An important element of your stewardship to God is the way that you choose to spend the time He has entrusted to you. Each waking moment holds the potential to help a friend or aid a stranger, to say a kind word or think a noble thought or offer a heartfelt prayer. Your challenge, as a believer, is to value your time, to use it judiciously, and to use it in ways that honor your Heavenly Father.

As you establish priorities for your day and your life, remember that each new day is a special treasure to be savored and celebrated.

As a Christian, you have much to celebrate and much to do. It's up to you, and you alone, to honor God for the gift of time by using that gift wisely. Every day, like every life, is composed of moments. Each moment of your life holds within it the potential to seek God's will and to serve His purposes. If you are wise, you will strive to do both.

How will you invest your time today? Will you savor the moments of your life, or will you squander them? Will you use your time as an instrument of God's will, or will you allow commonplace distractions to rule your day and your life?

The gift of time is indeed a gift from God. Treat it as if it were a precious, fleeting, one-of-a-kind treasure. Because it is.

Life's unfolding stops for no one.

Kathy Troccoli

Values for Life

It's Up To You: Finding time for God takes time . . . and it's up to you to find it. The world is constantly vying for your attention, and sometimes the noise can be deafening. Remember the words of Elisabeth Elliot; she said, "The world is full of noise. Let us learn the art of silence, stillness, and solitude."

Timeless Wisdom for Godly Living

God has a present will for your life. It is neither chaotic nor utterly exhausting. In the midst of many good choices vying for your time, He will give you the discernment to recognize what is best.

Beth Moore

To choose time is to save time.

Francis Bacon

So teach us to number our days,
that we may gain a heart of wisdom.
Psalm 90:12 NKJV

The best use of life is love. The best expression of love is time. The best time to love is now.

Rick Warren

Our time is short! The time we can invest for God, in creative things, in receiving our fellowmen for Christ, is short!

Billy Graham

As we surrender the use of our time to the lordship of Christ, He will lead us to use it in the most productive way imaginable.

Charles Stanley

More Words from God's Word

*To every thing there is a season, and a time to every purpose under
the heaven: A time to be born, and a time to die; a time to plant,
and a time to pluck up that which is planted; A time to kill, and
a time to heal; a time to break down, and a time to build up;
A time to weep, and a time to laugh; a time to mourn, and a time to
dance; A time to cast away stones, and a time to gather stones together;
a time to embrace, and a time to refrain from embracing; A time to get,
and a time to lose; a time to keep, and a time to cast away; A time to
rend, and a time to sew; a time to keep silence, and a time to speak;
A time to love, and a time to hate; a time of war, and a time of peace.*

Ecclesiastes 3:1-8 KJV

My Values for Life

	Check Your Value	
High	Med.	Low

I understand the importance of setting priorities.

— — —

I believe that time is a nonrenewable resource that can
be invested or squandered.

— — —

I understand that one form of stewardship is the
stewardship of my time.

— — —

Directing Our Thoughts

Summing it all up, friends, I'd say you'll do best by filling your minds and meditating on things true, noble, reputable, authentic, compelling, gracious, the best, not the worst; the beautiful, not the ugly; things to praise, not things to curse. Put into practice what you learned from me, what you heard and saw and realized. Do that, and God, who makes everything work together, will work you into his most excellent harmonies.

Philippians 4:8-9 MSG

Our thoughts have the power to shape our lives—for better or worse. Thoughts have the power to lift our spirits, to improve our circumstances, and to strengthen our relationship with the Creator. But, our thoughts also have the power to cause us great harm if we focus too intently upon those things that distance us from God.

How will you direct your thoughts today? Will you obey the words of Philippians 4:8 by dwelling upon those things that are honorable, true, and worthy of praise? Or will you allow your thoughts to be hijacked by the negativity that seems to dominate our troubled world?

Are you fearful, angry, bored, or worried? Are you so preoccupied with the concerns of this day that you fail to thank God for the promise of eternity? Are you confused, bitter, or pessimistic? If so, God wants to have a little talk with you.

God intends that you experience joy and abundance, but He will not force His joy upon you; you must claim it for yourself. It's up to you to celebrate the life that God has given you by focusing your mind upon "whatever is of good repute." Today, spend more time thinking about your blessings, and less time fretting about your hardships. Then, take time to thank the Giver of all things good for gifts that are, in truth, far too numerous to count.

If our minds are stayed upon God, His peace will rule the affairs entertained by our minds. If, on the other hand, we allow our minds to dwell on the cares of this world, God's peace will be far from our thoughts.

Woodroll Kroll

Values for Life

Good thoughts create good deeds. Good thoughts lead to good deeds, and bad thoughts lead elsewhere. So guard your thoughts accordingly.

Timeless Wisdom for Godly Living

Occupy your minds with good thoughts, or the enemy will fill them with bad ones. Unoccupied, they cannot be.

St. Thomas More

No more imperfect thoughts. No more sad memories. No more ignorance. My redeemed body will have a redeemed mind. Grant me a foretaste of that perfect mind as you mirror your thoughts in me today.

Joni Eareckson Tada

Those who are pure in their thinking are happy, because they will be with God.
Matthew 5:8 NCV

The things we think are the things that feed our souls. If we think on pure and lovely things, we shall grow pure and lovely like them; and the converse is equally true.

Hannah Whitall Smith

Your thoughts are the determining factor as to whose mold you are conformed to. Control your thoughts and you control the direction of your life.

Charles Stanley

More Words from God's Word

Come near to God, and God will come near to you. You sinners, clean sin out of your lives. You who are trying to follow God and the world at the same time, make your thinking pure.

James 4:8 NCV

Set your mind on things above, not on things on the earth.

Colossians 3:2 NKJV

So think clearly and exercise self-control. Look forward to the special blessings that will come to you at the return of Jesus Christ.

1 Peter 1:13 NLT

May the words of my mouth and the thoughts of my heart be pleasing to you, O LORD, my rock and my redeemer.

Psalm 19:14 NLT

My Values for Life

	Check Your Value	
High	Med.	Low

I understand the importance of directing my thoughts in a proper direction.

— — —

I believe that emotions are contagious, so I try to associate with people who are upbeat, optimistic, and encouraging.

— — —

I understand that when I dwell on positive thoughts, I feel better about myself and my circumstances.

— — —

Materialism 101: The Value of Stuff

*Yes, a person is a fool to store up earthly wealth but not have
a rich relationship with God.*

Luke 12:21 NLT

Is "shop till you drop" your motto? Hopefully not. On the grand stage of a well-lived life, material possessions should play a rather small role. Of course, we all need the basic necessities of life, but once we meet those needs, the piling up of stuff creates more problems than it solves.

Our society is in love with money and the things that money can buy. God is not. God cares about people, not possessions, and so must we. We must, to the best of our abilities, love our neighbors as ourselves, and we must, to the best of our abilities, resist the mighty temptation to place possessions ahead of people.

How much stuff is too much stuff? Well, if your desire for stuff is getting in the way of your desire to know God, then you've got too much stuff—it's as simple as that.

If you find yourself wrapped up in the concerns of the material world, it's time to reorder your priorities by turning your thoughts to more important matters. And, it's time to begin storing up riches that will endure throughout eternity: the spiritual kind. Money, in and of itself, is not evil; worshipping money is. So today, as you prioritize matters of importance in your life, remember that God is almighty, but the dollar is not.

As faithful stewards of what we have, ought we not to give earnest thought to our staggering surplus?

Elisabeth Elliot

Values for Life

Materialism Made Simple: The world wants you to believe that "money and stuff" can buy happiness. Don't believe it! Genuine happiness comes not from money, but from the things that money can't buy—starting, of course, with your relationship to God and His only begotten Son.

Timeless Wisdom for Godly Living

If you want to be truly happy, you won't find it on an endless quest for more stuff. You'll find it in receiving God's generosity and the passing that generosity along.

Bill Hybels

It's sobering to contemplate how much time, effort, sacrifice, compromise, and attention we give to acquiring and increasing our supply of something that is totally insignificant in eternity.

Anne Graham Lotz

For where your treasure is, there your heart will be also.
Luke 12:34 NKJV

There is absolutely no evidence that complexity and materialism lead to happiness. On the contrary, there is plenty of evidence that simplicity and spirituality lead to joy, a blessedness that is better than happiness.

Dennis Swanberg

When we put people before possessions in our hearts, we are sowing seeds of enduring satisfaction.

Beverly LaHaye

Getting a little greedy? Pray without seizing.

Anonymous

More Words from God's Word

For what will it profit a man if he gains the whole world, and loses his own soul? Or what will a man give in exchange for his soul?

Mark 8:36-37 NKJV

Lay not up for yourselves treasures upon earth, where moth and rust doth corrupt, and where thieves break through and steal: but lay up for yourselves treasures in heaven, where neither moth nor rust doth corrupt, and where thieves do not break through nor steal:for where your treasure is, there will your heart be also.

Matthew 6:19-21 KJV

No one can serve two masters. The person will hate one master and love the other, or will follow one master and refuse to follow the other. You cannot serve both God and worldly riches.

Matthew 6:24 NCV

My Values for Life

	Check Your Value	
High	Med.	Low

I don't expect material possessions to bring me lasting happiness.

I believe that my possessions are actually God's possessions, so I try to use them for His purposes.

My spending habits reflect the values that I hold dear, so I try my best to be a faithful steward of my resources.

The Wisdom of Thanksgiving

It is good to give thanks to the Lord, to sing praises to the Most High.
It is good to proclaim your unfailing love in the morning,
your faithfulness in the evening.

Psalm 92:1-2 NLT

Are you basically a thankful person? Do you appreciate the stuff you've got and the life that you're privileged to live? You most certainly should be thankful. After all, when you stop to think about it, God has given you more blessings than you can count. So the question of the day is this: will you slow down long enough to thank your Heavenly Father . . . or not?

Sometimes, life here on earth can be complicated, demanding, and frustrating. When the demands of life leave you rushing from place to place with scarcely a moment to spare, you may fail to pause and thank your Creator for the countless blessings He has given you. Failing to thank God is understandable . . . but it's wrong.

God's Word makes it clear: a wise heart is a thankful heart. Period. Your Heavenly Father has blessed you beyond measure, and you owe Him everything, including your thanks. God is always listening—are you willing to say thanks? It's up to you, and the next move is yours.

God has promised that if we harvest well with the tools of thanksgiving, there will be seeds for planting in the spring.

Gloria Gaither

The joy of the Holy Spirit is experienced by giving thanks in all situations.

Bill Bright

Values for Life

When is the best time to say "thanks" to God? Any time. God loves you all the time, and that's exactly why you should praise Him all the time.

Timeless Wisdom for Godly Living

When it comes to life, the critical thing is whether you take things for granted or take them with gratitude.

G. K. Chesterton

It is always possible to be thankful for what is given rather than to complain about what is not given. One or the other becomes a habit of life.

Elisabeth Elliot

Is anyone happy? Let him sing songs of praise.
James 5:13 NIV

Go outside, to the fields, enjoy nature and the sunshine, go out and try to recapture happiness in yourself and in God. Think of all the beauty that's still left in and around you and be happy!

Anne Frank

We ought to give thanks for all fortune: if it is good, because it is good, if bad, because it works in us patience, humility, and the contempt of this world along with the hope of our eternal country.

C. S. Lewis

More Words from God's Word

Let the Word of Christ—the Message—have the run of the house. Give it plenty of room in your lives. Instruct and direct one another using good common sense. And sing, sing your hearts out to God! Let every detail in your lives—words, actions, whatever—be done in the name of the Master, Jesus, thanking God the Father every step of the way.

Colossians 3:16-17 MSG

Our prayers for you are always spilling over into thanksgivings. We can't quit thanking God our Father and Jesus our Messiah for you!

Colossians 1:3 MSG

Give thanks in all circumstances; for this is God's will for you in Christ Jesus.

1 Thessalonians 5:18 NIV

My Values for Life

I understand that I should never take my blessings for granted.

I understand the importance of remaining humble as I praise God and thank Him for His gifts.

I will not only thank God for His gifts, I will use those gifts as one way of honoring Him.

Check Your Value		
High	Med.	Low
—	—	—
—	—	—
—	—	—

A Compelling Testimony: Yours

You are the light of the world. A city that is set on a hill cannot be hidden.
Nor do they light a lamp and put it under a basket,
but on a lampstand, and it gives light to all who are in the house.
Let your light so shine before men, that they may see your good works
and glorify your Father in heaven.

Matthew 5:14-16 NKJV

Let's face facts: those of us who are Christians should be willing to talk about the things that Christ has done for us. Our personal testimonies are vitally important, but sometimes, because of shyness or insecurities, we're afraid to share our experiences. And that's unfortunate.

In his second letter to Timothy, Paul shares a message to believers of every generation when he writes, "God has not given us a spirit of timidity" (1:7). Paul's meaning is crystal clear: When sharing our testimonies, we must be courageous and unashamed.

We live in a world that desperately needs the healing message of Christ Jesus. Every believer, each in his or her own way, bears responsibility for sharing the Good News of our Savior. And it is important to remember that we bear testimony through both words and actions.

If you seek to be a faithful follower of Christ, then it's time for you to share your testimony with others. So today, preach the Gospel through your words and your deeds . . . but not necessarily in that order.

It's a joy to share my faith.
I've found something so special that I want others to share in it. When something is that close to your heart, share it.

Michael Chang

Values for Life

Today, I Will Think About . . . The importance of sharing my testimony through my words and my actions.

Timeless Wisdom for Godly Living

A man who lives right, and is right, has more power in his silence than another has by his words.

Phillips Brooks

Faith in small things has repercussions that ripple all the way out. In a huge, dark room a little match can light up the place.

Joni Eareckson Tada

> *Whoever acknowledges me before men, I will also acknowledge him before my Father in heaven.*
> Matthew 10:32 NIV

There is nothing more appealing or convincing to a watching world than to hear the testimony of someone who has just been with Jesus.

Henry Blackaby

Theology is an interesting school of thought. The Bible is beautiful literature. Sitting in a quiet sanctuary, bathed in the amber light from stained-glass windows, having our jangled nerves soothed by the chords from an organ—all that is inspiring. But to tell you the truth, when we leave the classroom, close the church door, and walk out into the real world, it is the indisputable proof of changed lives that makes us believers.

Gloria Gaither

More Words from God's Word

But as for me, I will never boast about anything except the cross of our Lord Jesus Christ, through whom the world has been crucified to me, and I to the world.

Galatians 6:14 HCSB

Be wise in the way you act with people who are not believers, making the most of every opportunity.

Colossians 4:5 NCV

But when the Holy Spirit has come upon you, you will receive power and will tell people about me everywhere—in Jerusalem, throughout Judea, in Samaria, and to the ends of the earth.

Acts 1:8 NLT

So proclaim the Message with intensity; keep on your watch. Challenge, warn, and urge your people. Don't ever quit. Just keep it simple.

2 Timothy 4:2 MSG

My Values for Life

| Check Your Value | | |
High	Med.	Low

I believe that it is important to share my testimony.

I feel that my actions are as much a part of my testimony as my words.

I feel that my testimony has the power to change the world.

The Value of Your Daily Devotional

*Stay clear of silly stories that get dressed up as religion.
Exercise daily in God—no spiritual flabbiness, please!*

1 Timothy 4:7 MSG

Each day has 1,440 minutes—do you value your relationship with God enough to spend a few of those minutes with Him? He deserves that much of your time and more—is He receiving it from you? Hopefully so. But if you find that you're simply "too busy" for a daily chat with your Father in heaven, it's time to take a long, hard look at your priorities and your values.

As you consider your plans for the day ahead, here's a tip: organize your life around this simple principle: "God first." When you place your Creator where He belongs—at the very center of your day and your life—the rest of your priorities will fall into place.

Each new day is a gift from God, and if you are wise, you will spend a few quiet moments each morning thanking the Giver. Daily life is woven together with the threads of habit, and no habit is more important to your spiritual health than the discipline of daily prayer and devotion to the Creator.

Warren Wiersbe writes, "Surrender your mind to the Lord at the beginning of each day." And that's sound advice. When you begin each day with your head bowed and your heart lifted, you are reminded of God's love, His protection, and His commandments. Then, you can align your priorities for the coming day with the teachings and commandments that God has placed upon your heart.

So, if you've acquired the unfortunate habit of trying to "squeeze" God into the corners of your life, it's time to reshuffle the items on your to-do list by placing God first. God wants your undivided attention, not the leftovers of your day. And if you haven't already done so, form the habit of spending quality time with your Father in heaven. He deserves it . . . and so, for that matter, do you.

Make a plan now to keep a daily appointment with God. The enemy is going to tell you to set it aside, but you must carve out the time. If you're too busy to meet with the Lord, friend, then you are simply too busy.

Charles Swindoll

Values for Life

How much time can you spare? Decide how much of your time God deserves, and then give it to Him. Don't organize your day so that God gets "what's left." Give Him what you honestly believe He deserves.

Timeless Wisdom for Godly Living

We all need to make time for God. Even Jesus made time to be alone with the Father.

Kay Arthur

We must appropriate the tender mercy of God every day after conversion, or problems quickly develop. We need his grace daily in order to live a righteous life.

Jim Cymbala

It is good to give thanks to the Lord, to sing praises to the Most High. It is good to proclaim your unfailing love in the morning, your faithfulness in the evening.
Psalm 92:1-2 NLT

God is a place of safety you can run to, but it helps if you are running to Him on a daily basis so that you are in familiar territory.

Stormie Omartian

The moment you wake up each morning, all your wishes and hopes for the day rush at you like wild animals. And the first job each morning consists in shoving it all back; in listening to that other voice, taking that other point of view, letting that other, larger, stronger, quieter life coming flowing in.

C. S. Lewis

More Words from God's Word

Every morning he wakes me. He teaches me to listen like a student. The Lord God helps me learn . . . .

Isaiah 50:4-5 NCV

Be still, and know that I am God . . . .

Psalm 46:10 NKJV

In quietness and trust is your strength.

Isaiah 30:15 NASB

Let the words of my mouth and the meditation of my heart be acceptable in Your sight, O Lord, my strength and my Redeemer.

Psalm 19:14 NKJV

My Values for Life

I understand the importance of spending time each day with God.

I have a regular time and place where I can read, pray, and talk to God.

I try to listen carefully to the things that God places upon my heart.

Check Your Value		
High	Med.	Low
—	—	—
—	—	—
—	—	—

A Lifetime of Spiritual Growth

Long for the pure milk of the word,
so that by it you may grow in respect to salvation.

1 Peter 2:2 NASB

When it comes to your faith, God doesn't intend for you to stand still. He wants you to keep moving and growing. In fact, God's plan for you includes a lifetime of prayer, praise, and spiritual growth.

When we cease to grow, either emotionally or spiritually, we do ourselves and our loved ones a profound disservice. But, if we study God's Word, if we obey His commandments, and if we live in the center of His will, we will not be "stagnant" believers; we will, instead, be growing Christians . . . and that's exactly what God wants for our lives.

Many of life's most important lessons are painful to learn. During times of heartbreak and hardship, we must be courageous and we must be patient, knowing that in His own time, God will heal us if we invite Him into our hearts.

Spiritual growth need not take place only in times of adversity. We must seek to grow in our knowledge and love of the Lord every day that we live. In those quiet moments when we open our hearts to God, the One who made us keeps remaking us. He gives us direction, perspective, wisdom, and courage. The appropriate moment to accept those spiritual gifts is the present one.

Are you as mature as you're ever going to be? Hopefully not! When it comes to your faith, God doesn't intend for you to become "fully grown," at least not in this lifetime. In fact, God still has important lessons that He intends to teach you. So ask yourself this: what lesson is God trying to teach me today? And then go about the business of learning it.

We only grow by taking risks, and the most difficult risk of all is to be honest with ourselves and with others.

Rick Warren

Values for Life

How do I know if I can still keep growing as a Christian? Check your pulse. If it's still beating, then you can still keep growing.

Timeless Wisdom for Godly Living

Our progress in holiness depends on God and ourselves—on God's grace and on our will to be holy.

Mother Teresa

We look at our burdens and heavy loads, and we shrink from them. But, if we lift them and bind them about our hearts, they become wings, and on them we can rise and soar toward God.

Mrs. Charles E. Cowman

We grow spiritually as our Lord grew physically: by a life of simple, unobtrusive obedience.

Oswald Chambers

This is why I remind you to keep using the gift God gave you when I laid my hands on you. Now let it grow, as a small flame grows into a fire.
2 Timothy 1:6 NCV

Salvation is the process that's done, that's secure, that no one can take away from you. Sanctification is the lifelong process of being changed from one degree of glory to the next, growing in Christ, putting away the old, taking on the new.

Max Lucado

More Words from God's Word

*The lines of purpose in your lives never grow slack, tightly tied as they
are to your future in heaven, kept taut by hope. It's the same all over the
world. The Message bears fruit and gets larger and stronger, just as it has
in you. From the very first day you heard and recognized the truth of what
God is doing, you've been hungry for more.*

Colossians 1:5-6 MSG

*And I pray that you and all God's holy people will have the power to
understand the greatness of Christ's love—how wide and how long and
how high and how deep that love is. Christ's love is greater than anyone
can ever know, but I pray that you will be able to know that love. Then
you can be filled with the fullness of God.*

Ephesians 3:18-19 NCV

My Values for Life

I believe that the level of my spiritual maturity has a
direct impact, either positively or negatively,
on those around me.

Since I believe that I still have "room to grow" in my
faith, gaining spiritual maturity remains a priority for me.

Since I feel that spiritual growth happens day by day,
I will live, worship, and pray accordingly.

Check Your Value		
High	Med.	Low
—	—	—
—	—	—
—	—	—

Spiritual Growth

Speaking with a Voice of Triumph

For you made us only a little lower than God,
and you crowned us with glory and honor.

Psalm 8:5 NLT

re you your own worst critic? If so, it's time to become a little more understanding of the person you see whenever you look into the mirror.

Millions of words have been written about various ways to improve self-image and increase self-esteem. Yet, maintaining a healthy self-image is, to a surprising extent, a matter of doing three things: (1) Obeying God (2) Thinking healthy thoughts (3) Finding a purpose for your life that pleases your Creator and yourself.

The following common-sense, Biblically-based tips can help you build the kind of self-image—and the kind of life—that both you and God can be proud of:

Do the right thing: If you're misbehaving, how can you possibly hope to feel good about yourself? (See Romans 14:12)

Watch what you think: If your inner voice is, in reality, your inner critic, you need to tone down the criticism now. And while you're at it, train yourself to begin thinking thoughts that are more rational, more accepting, and less judgmental. (Philippians 4:8)

Spend time with boosters, not critics: Are your friends putting you down? If so, find new friends. (Hebrews 3:13)

Find something that you're passionate about: Become so busy following your passion that you forget to worry about your self-esteem. (Colossians 3:23)

Don't worry too much about self-esteem: Instead, worry more about living a life that is pleasing to God. Learn to think optimistically. Find a worthy purpose. Find people to love and people to serve. When you do, your self-esteem will, on most days, take care of itself.

Whether we find ourselves overworking, overspending, overparenting—whatever we choose as our obsession—there is a valuable freedom found when we can accept that our worth is not based on what we do, how we do it, or what others think of us.

Annie Chapman

Values for Life

You are incredibly special to God . . . Are you incredibly special to yourself?

Timeless Wisdom for Godly Living

Stop blaming yourself and feeling guilty, unworthy, and unloved. Instead begin to say, "If God is for me, who can be against me? God loves me, and I love myself. Praise the Lord, I am free in Jesus' name, amen!"

Joyce Meyer

You're blessed when you're content with just who you are—no more, no less. That's the moment you find yourselves proud owners of everything that can't be bought.

Matthew 5:5 MSG

Your core identity—and particularly your perception of it—plays a vital role in determining how you carry yourself in daily life, how much joy you experience, how you treat other people, and how you respond to God.

Josh McDowell

Your self-image need not be permanently damaged by the circumstances of life. It can be recast when there is an infusion of new life in Jesus Christ.

Ed Young

More Words from God's Word

God began doing a good work in you, and I am sure he will continue it until it is finished when Jesus Christ comes again.

Philippians 1:6 NCV

For You formed my inward parts; You covered me in my mother's womb. I will praise You, for I am fearfully and wonderfully made; Marvelous are Your works.

Psalm 139:13-14 NKJV

Blessed is the man who does not condemn himself.

Romans 14:22 HCSB

And the work of righteousness will be peace, And the service of righteousness, quietness and confidence forever.

Isaiah 32:17 NASB

My Values for Life

Because I know that God loves me, I believe that I should love myself.

I trust that God is working in me and through me to help me become the person He intends for me to be.

I believe that one reason to study God's Word is this: It tells me what God thinks of my life.

Check Your Value		
High	Med.	Low
—	—	—
—	—	—
—	—	—

Character-building 101

The integrity of the upright guides them,
but the unfaithful are destroyed by their duplicity.

Proverbs 11:3 NIV

Catherine Marshall correctly observed, "The single most important element in any human relationship is honesty—with oneself, with God, and with others." Godly men and women agree. As believers in Christ, we must seek to live each day with discipline, honesty, and faith. When we do, at least two things happen: integrity becomes a habit, and God blesses us because of our obedience to Him. Living a life of integrity isn't always the easiest way, but it is always the right way . . . and God clearly intends that it should be our way, too.

Character isn't built overnight; it is built slowly over a lifetime. It is the sum of every right decision and every honest word. It is forged on the anvil of honorable work and polished by the twin virtues of honesty and fairness. Character is a precious thing—difficult to build and wonderful to behold.

Oswald Chambers, the author of the Christian classic *My Utmost for His Highest*, advised, "Never support an experience which does not have God as its source, and faith in God as its result." These words serve as a powerful reminder that as Christians we are called to walk with God and to obey His commandments. But, we live in a world that presents us with countless temptations to wander far from God's path. These temptations have the potential to destroy us, in part, because they cause us to be dishonest with ourselves and with others.

Dishonesty is a habit. Once we start bending the truth, we're likely to keep bending it. A far better strategy, of course, is to acquire the habit of being completely forthright with God, with other people, and with ourselves.

Honesty is also a habit, a habit that pays powerful dividends for those who place character above convenience. So, the next time you're tempted to bend the truth—or to break it—ask yourself this simple question: "What does God want to do?" Then listen carefully to your conscience. When you do, your actions will be honorable, and your character will take care of itself.

Every secret act of character, conviction, and courage has been observed in living color by our omniscient God.

Bill Hybels

Values for Life

One of your greatest possessions is integrity . . . don't lose it. Billy Graham was right when he said: "Integrity is the glue that holds our way of life together. We must constantly strive to keep our integrity intact. When wealth is lost, nothing is lost; when health is lost, something is lost; when character is lost, all is lost."

Timeless Wisdom for Godly Living

Your true character is something that no one can injure but yourself.

C. H. Spurgeon

If I take care of my character, my reputation will take care of itself.

D. L. Moody

> *Applying all diligence, in your faith*
> *supply moral excellence.*
> *2 Peter 1:5 NASB*

It is the thoughts and intents of the heart that shape a person's life.

John Eldredge

Sow an act, and you reap a habit. Sow a habit and you reap a character. Sow a character and you reap a destiny.

Anonymous

Image is what people think we are; integrity is what we really are.

John Maxwell

More Words from God's Word

A good name is more desirable than great riches; to be esteemed is better than silver or gold.

Proverbs 22:1 NIV

We also have joy with our troubles, because we know that these troubles produce patience. And patience produces character, and character produces hope.

Romans 5:3-4 NCV

In everything set them an example by doing what is good. In your teaching show integrity, seriousness and soundness of speech that cannot be condemned, so that those who oppose you may be ashamed because they have nothing bad to say about us.

Titus 2:7 NIV

My Values for Life

	Check Your Value	
High	Med.	Low

I believe that character matters.

| — | — | — |

I try to do the right thing because I have to live with myself.

| — | — | — |

I understand that my power to witness for Christ depends upon my actions as well as upon my words.

| — | — | — |

Making All Things New

Therefore, this is what the Lord says:
If you return, I will restore you; you will stand in My presence.

Jeremiah 15:19 HCSB

ven the most inspired Christian teenagers can find themselves running on empty. Even people with the best intentions can run out of energy; even the most hopeful believers can be burdened by fears and doubts. And you're no exception.

When you're exhausted or worried, there is a source from which you can draw the power needed to recharge your spiritual batteries. That source is God.

God intends that His children lead joyous lives filled with abundance and peace. But sometimes, abundance and peace seem very far away. During these difficult days, we must turn to God for renewal, and when we do, He will restore us.

Are you tired or troubled? Turn your heart toward God in prayer. Are you weak or worried? Take the time—or, more accurately, make the time—to delve deeply into God's Holy Word. Are you spiritually depleted? Call upon fellow believers to support you, and call upon Christ to renew your spirit and your life. When you do, you'll discover that the Creator of the universe stands always ready and always able to create a new sense of wonderment and joy in you.

But while relaxation is one thing, refreshment is another. We need to drink frequently and at length from God's fresh springs, to spend time in the Scripture, time in fellowship with Him, time worshiping Him.

Ruth Bell Graham

Values for Life

God wants to give you peace, and He wants to renew your spirit. It's up to you to slow down and give Him a chance to do it.

Renewal

Timeless Wisdom for Godly Living

I wish I could make it all new again; I can't. But God can. "He restores my soul," wrote the shepherd. God doesn't reform; he restores. He doesn't camouflage the old; he restores the new. The Master Builder will pull out the original plan and restore it. He will restore the vigor, he will restore the energy. He will restore the hope. He will restore the soul.

Max Lucado

In those desperate times when we feel like we don't have an ounce of strength, He will gently pick up our heads so that our eyes can behold something—something that will keep His hope alive in us.

Kathy Troccoli

*I will give you a new heart
and put a new spirit within you.*
Ezekiel 36:26 HCSB

One reason so much American Christianity is a mile wide and an inch deep is that Christians are simply tired. Sometimes you need to kick back and rest for Jesus' sake.

Dennis Swanberg

If the pace and the push, the noise and the crowds are getting to you, it's time to stop the nonsense and find a place of solace to refresh your spirit.

Charles Swindoll

More Words from God's Word

Do you not know? Have you not heard? The Everlasting God, the LORD, the Creator of the ends of the earth does not become weary or tired. His understanding is inscrutable. He gives strength to the weary, and to him who lacks might He increases power. Though youths grow weary and tired, and vigorous young men stumble badly, yet those who wait for the LORD will gain new strength; they will mount up with wings like eagles, they will run and not get tired, they will walk and not become weary.

Isaiah 40:28-31 NASB

Be energetic in your life of salvation, reverent and sensitive before God. That energy is God's energy, an energy deep within you, God himself willing and working at what will give him the most pleasure.

Philippians 2:12-13 MSG

My Values for Life

I believe that God can make all things new . . . including me.

I take time each day to be still and let God give me perspective and direction.

I understand the importance of getting a good night's sleep.

Check Your Value		
High	Med.	Low
—	—	—
—	—	—
—	—	—

Renewal

Too Many Questions?

*We are pressured in every way but not crushed;
we are perplexed but not in despair.*

2 Corinthians 4:8 HCSB

Have you ever read the story about Moses trying to lead his people by following the will of God? If so, then you can plainly see that even a good man like Moses couldn't always understand the mysteries of God's plans. And neither can we. Sometimes, people who do nothing wrong get sick; sometimes, innocent people are hurt; sometimes, bad things happen to very good people. And just like Moses, we can't always understand why.

God doesn't explain Himself to us with the clarity that we humans would prefer (think about this: if God did explain Himself with perfect clarity, we wouldn't have enough brainpower to understand the explanation that He gave!).

When innocent people are hurt, we question God because we can't figure out exactly what He's doing, or why. Why are innocent people allowed to feel pain and good people allowed to die? Since we can't fully answer those kinds of questions now, we must trust in God's love, God's wisdom, and God's plan.

And while we're waiting for that wonderful day (in heaven) when all our questions will be answered, we should use the time that we have here on earth to help the people who need it most. After all, we'll have plenty of time to have our questions answered when we get to heaven. But when it comes to helping our neighbors, we don't have nearly that much time. So let's get busy helping . . . right now!

Be to the world a sign that while we as Christians do not have all the answers, we do know and care about the questions.

Billy Graham

Values for Life

Too many questions? If you're faced with too many questions and too few answers, talk to God about it. When you do, you'll discover that He has more answers than you have questions.

Timeless Wisdom for Godly Living

When there is perplexity there is always guidance—not always at the moment we ask, but in good time, which is God's time. There is no need to fret and stew.

Elisabeth Elliot

We are finding we don't have such a gnawing need to know the answers when we know the Answer.

Gloria Gaither

Questions never threaten the living God, who is constantly calling us, and who affirms for us that love is stronger than hate, blessing stronger than cursing.

Madeleine L'Engle

Trust the Lord with all your heart,
and don't depend on your own understanding.
Proverbs 3:5 NCV

The Christian call . . . does not mean we are to become rigid and aggressive moralists with a strict and firm answer to every ethical problem. But it does mean we are committed to the conviction that there is an answer to be found.

David H. C. Read

More Words from God's Word

Can you understand the secrets of God? His limits are higher than the heavens; you cannot reach them! They are deeper than the grave; you cannot understand them! His limits are longer than the earth and wider than the sea.

Job 11:7-9 NCV

We don't yet see things clearly. We're squinting in a fog, peering through a mist. But it won't be long before the weather clears and the sun shines bright! We'll see it all then, see it all as clearly as God sees us, knowing him directly just as he knows us! But for right now, until that completeness, we have three things to do to lead us toward that consummation: Trust steadily in God, hope unswervingly, love extravagantly. And the best of the three is love.

1 Corinthians 13:12-13 MSG

My Values for Life

When I have questions, I believe that it is important to take those questions to the Lord.

Even when I cannot understand why certain things happen, I trust God's plan for my life and the world.

As a way of dealing with my questions and worries, I find that I am helped by Bible study, prayer, and worship.

Check Your Value		
High	Med.	Low
—	—	—
—	—	—
—	—	—

The Right Thing to Do

But prove yourselves doers of the word, and not merely hearers.

James 1:22 NASB

If you're like most people, you seek the admiration of your friends and acquaintances. But the eagerness to please others should never overshadow your eagerness to please God. If you seek to fulfill the purposes that God has in store for you, then you must be a "doer of the word." And how can you do so? By putting God first.

The words of Matthew 6:33 make it clear: "But seek first the kingdom of God and His righteousness, and all these things will be provided for you" (HCSB). God has given you a priceless guidebook, an indispensable tool for "seeking His kingdom." That tool, of course, is the Holy Bible. It contains thorough instructions which, if followed, lead to fulfillment, righteousness, and salvation.

But for those who would ignore God's Word, Martin Luther issued this stern warning: "You may as well quit reading and hearing the Word of God and give it to the devil if you do not desire to live according to it." Luther understood that obedience leads to abundance just as surely as disobedience leads to disaster; you should understand it, too.

Each new day presents countless opportunities to put God in

first place . . . or not. When you honor Him by living according to His commandments, you earn the abundance and peace that He promises. But, if you ignore God's teachings, you will inevitably bring needless suffering upon yourself and your family.

Would you like a time-tested formula for successful living? Here it is: Don't just listen to God's Word; live by it. Does this sound too simple? Perhaps it is simple, but it is also the only way to reap the marvelous riches that God has in store for you.

> The best evidence of our having the truth is our walking in the truth.
>
> *Matthew Henry*

Values for Life

Obey God or face the consequences: God rewards obedience and punishes disobedience. It's not enough to understand God's rules; you must also live by them . . . or else.

Timeless Wisdom for Godly Living

Resolved: never to do anything which I should be afraid to do if it were the last hour of my life.

Jonathan Edwards

> *By this we know that we have come to know Him, if we keep His commandments.*
>
> *1 John 2:3 NASB*

Righteousness not only defines God, but God defines righteousness.

Bill Hybels

Christians are the citizens of heaven, and while we are on earth, we ought to behave like heaven's citizens.

Warren Wiersbe

What you do reveals what you believe about God, regardless of what you say. When God reveals what He has purposed to do, you face a crisis—a decision time. God and the world can tell from your response what you really believe about God.

Henry Blackaby

If we have the true love of God in our hearts, we will show it in our lives. We will not have to go up and down the earth proclaiming it. We will show it in everything we say or do.

D. L. Moody

More Words from God's Word

But now you must be holy in everything you do, just as God—who chose you to be his children—is holy. For he himself has said, "You must be holy because I am holy."

1 Peter 1:15-16 NLT

Walk in a manner worthy of the God who calls you into His own kingdom and glory.

1 Thessalonians 2:12 NASB

Discipline yourself for the purpose of godliness.

1 Timothy 4:7 NASB

The LORD has sought out for Himself a man after His own heart.

2 Samuel 13:14 NASB

My Values for Life

I understand that my behavior reveals my relationship with God.

I understand that my behavior affects how I feel about myself.

I know that my behavior should reflect Biblical values.

Check Your Value		
High	Med.	Low
—	—	—
—	—	—
—	—	—

Putting Off Till Tomorrow

If you make a promise to God, don't be slow to keep it.
God is not happy with fools, so give God what you promised.

Ecclesiastes 5:4 NCV

When something important needs to be done, the best time to do it is sooner rather than later. But sometimes, instead of doing the smart thing (which, by the way, is choosing "sooner"), we may choose "later." When we do, we may pay a heavy price for our shortsightedness.

The habit of procrastination takes a twofold toll on its victims. First, important work goes unfinished; second (and more importantly), valuable energy is wasted in the process of putting off the things that remain undone. Procrastination results from an individual's shortsighted attempt to postpone temporary discomfort. What results is a senseless cycle of (1) Delay, followed by (2) Worry, followed by (3) A panicky and futile attempt to "catch up." Procrastination is, at its core, a struggle against oneself; the only antidote is action.

Once you acquire the habit of doing what needs to be done when it needs to be done, you will avoid untold trouble, worry, and stress. So learn to defeat procrastination by paying less attention to your fears and more attention to your responsibilities.

Are you one of those people who put things off till the last minute? If so, it's time to change your ways. Whatever "it" is, do it now. When you do, you won't have to worry about "it" later.

I've found that the worst thing I can do when it comes to any kind of potential pressure situation is to put off dealing with it.

John Maxwell

Values for Life

If unpleasant work needs to be done, do it sooner rather than later . . . It's easy to put off unpleasant tasks until "later." A far better strategy is this: Do the unpleasant work first so you can enjoy the rest of the day.

Timeless Wisdom for Godly Living

Don't duck the most difficult problems. That just insures that the hardest part will be left when you're most tired. Get the big one done, and it's all downhill from then on.

Norman Vincent Peale

Not now becomes never.

Martin Luther

If you are too lazy to plow in the right season, you will have no food at the harvest.

Proverbs 20:4 NLT

Never fail to do something because you don't feel like it. Sometimes you just have to do it now, and you'll feel like it later.

Marie T. Freeman

Nothing would be done at all, if a man waited until he could do it so well that no one could find fault with it.

John Henry Cardinal Newman

Character is formed by doing the thing we are supposed to do, when it should be done, whether we feel like doing it or not.

Father Flanagan

More Words from God's Word

If you do nothing in a difficult time, your strength is limited.

Proverbs 24:10 HCSB

But prove yourselves doers of the word, and not merely hearers who delude themselves.

James 1:22 NASB

Because the kingdom of God is present not in talk but in power.

1 Corinthians 4:20 NCV

Therefore, get your minds ready for action, being self-disciplined, and set your hope completely on the grace to be brought to you at the revelation of Jesus Christ.

1 Peter 1:13 HCSB

My Values for Life

I try to avoid the trap of procrastination because I know that procrastination is counterproductive to my own best interests.

I understand the importance of doing first things first, even if I'd rather be doing something else.

Since I believe that procrastination only delays the inevitable, I try to do things sooner rather than later.

Check Your Value		
High	Med.	Low
—	—	—
—	—	—
—	—	—

Putting Possessions in Proper Perspective

A pretentious, showy life is an empty life;
a plain and simple life is a full life.

Proverbs 13:7 MSG

Okay, be honest—are you in love with stuff? If so, you're headed for trouble, and fast. Why? Because no matter how much you love stuff, stuff won't love you back.

In the life of committed Christians, material possessions should play a rather small role. Of course, we all need the basic necessities of life, but once we meet those needs for ourselves and for our families, the piling up of possessions creates more problems than it solves. Our real riches, of course, are not of this world. We are never really rich until we are rich in spirit.

Martin Luther observed, "Many things I have tried to grasp and have lost. That which I have placed in God's hands I still have." His words apply to all of us. Our earthly riches are transitory; our spiritual riches are not.

Do you find yourself wrapped up in the concerns of the material world? If so, it's time to reorder your priorities by turning your thoughts and your prayers to more important matters. And, it's time to begin storing up riches that will endure throughout eternity: the spiritual kind.

Wealth is something entrusted to us by God, something God doesn't want us to trust. He wants us to trust Him.

Warren Wiersbe

Values for Life

Stuff 101: The world says, "Buy more stuff." God says, "Stuff isn't important." Believe God.

Timeless Wisdom for Godly Living

Not the goods of the world, but God. Not riches, but God. Not honors, but God. Not advancement, but God. God always and in everything.

Vincent Pallotti

I have held many things in my hands, and I have lost them all; but whatever I have placed in God's hands, that I still possess.

Corrie ten Boom

Can your wealth or all [your] physical exertion keep [you] from distress?
Job 36:19 HCSB

God may be in the process of pruning something out of your life at this very moment. If this is the case, don't fight it. Instead, welcome it, for His pruning will make you more fruitful and bring greater glory to the Father.

Rick Yohn

No one is truly happy if he has what he wants, but only if he wants something he should have.

St. Augustine

When possessions become our god, we become materialistic and greedy . . . and we forfeit our contentment and our joy.

Charles Swindoll

More Words from God's Word

For the love of money is a root of all kinds of evil, for which some have strayed from the faith in their greediness, and pierced themselves through with many sorrows. But you, O man of God, flee these things and pursue righteousness, godliness, faith, love, patience, gentleness.

1 Timothy 6:10-11 NKJV

Keep your lives free from the love of money, and be satisfied with what you have.

Hebrews 13:5 NCV

Then Jesus said to them, "Be careful and guard against all kinds of greed. Life is not measured by how much one owns."

Luke 12:15 NCV

My Values for Life

Every day I will work to make certain that my possessions don't possess me.

I believe it is important to place spiritual possessions above material ones.

I believe that my enjoyment of life has less to do with material possessions and more do with my relationships—beginning with my relationship to God.

Check Your Value		
High	Med.	Low
—	—	—
—	—	—
—	—	—

The Power of the Words We Speak

Watch the way you talk. Let nothing foul or dirty come out of your mouth. Say only what helps, each word a gift.

Ephesians 4:29 MSG

How much value do you place on the words you speak? Hopefully, you understand that your words have great power . . . because they most certainly do. If your words are encouraging, you can lift others up; if your words are hurtful, you can hold others back.

The Bible makes it clear that "Reckless words pierce like a sword, but the tongue of the wise brings healing" (Proverbs 12:18 NIV). So, if you hope to solve problems instead of starting them, you must measure your words carefully. But sometimes, you'll be tempted to speak first and think second (with decidedly mixed results).

When you're frustrated or tired, you may say things that would be better left unspoken. Whenever you lash out in anger, you forgo the wonderful opportunity to consider your thoughts before you give voice to them. When you speak impulsively, you may, quite unintentionally, injure others.

A far better strategy, of course, is to do the more difficult thing: to think first and to speak next. When you do so, you give yourself ample time to compose your thoughts and to consult our Creator (but not necessarily in that order!).

The Bible warns that you will be judged by the words you speak (Matthew 12:36-37). And, Ephesians 4:29 instructs you to make "each word a gift" (MSG). These passages make it clear that God cares very much about the things you say and the way you say them. And if God cares that much, so should you.

Do you seek to be a source of encouragement to others? Are you a beacon of hope to your friends and family? And, do you seek to be a worthy ambassador for Christ? If so, you must speak words that are worthy of your Savior. So avoid angry outbursts. Refrain from impulsive outpourings. Terminate tantrums. Instead, speak words of encouragement and hope to a world that desperately needs both.

Words. Do you fully understand their power? Can any of us really grasp the mighty force behind the things we say? Do we stop and think before we speak, considering the potency of the words we utter?

Joni Eareckson Tada

Values for Life

When in doubt, use the Golden Rule to help you decide what to say: If you wouldn't like for somebody to say it about you, don't say it about them!

Timeless Wisdom for Godly Living

A little kindly advice is better than a great deal of scolding.

Fanny Crosby

When you talk, choose the very same words that you would use if Jesus were looking over your shoulder. Because He is.

Marie T. Freeman

For out of the overflow of the heart the mouth speaks.
Matthew 12:34 NIV

Fill the heart with the love of Christ so that only truth and purity can come out of the mouth.

Warren Wiersbe

The battle of the tongue is won not in the mouth, but in the heart.

Annie Chapman

Perhaps we have been guilty of speaking against someone and have not realized how it may have hurt them. Then when someone speaks against us, we suddenly realize how deeply such words hurt, and we become sensitive to what we have done.

Theodore Epp

More Words from God's Word

Careless words stab like a sword, but wise words bring healing.

Proverbs 12:18 NCV

May the words of my mouth and the meditation of my heart be pleasing in your sight, O LORD, my Rock and my Redeemer.

Psalm 19:14 NIV

If you confess with your mouth, "Jesus is Lord," and believe in your heart that God raised him from the dead, you will be saved. For it is with your heart that you believe and are justified, and it is with your mouth that you confess and are saved.

Romans 10:9-10 NIV

A word aptly spoken is like apples of gold in settings of silver.

Proverbs 25:11 NIV

Kind words are like honey—sweet to the soul and healthy for the body.

Proverbs 16:24 NLT

My Values for Life

I believe that my words are important, so I try to think before I speak, not after.

Every day, I try to find at least one person to encourage.

I find that when I encourage others, I, too, am encouraged.

Check Your Value		
High	Med.	Low
___	___	___
___	___	___
___	___	___

Speech

The Size of Your Problems

All I'm doing right now, friends, is showing how these things pertain to Apollos and me so that you will learn restraint and not rush into making judgments without knowing all the facts. It is important to look at things from God's point of view. I would rather not see you inflating or deflating reputations based on mere hearsay.

1 Corinthians 4:6 MSG

Here's a riddle: What is it that is too unimportant to pray about yet too big for God to handle? The answer, of course, is: "nothing." Yet sometimes, when the challenges of the day seem overwhelming, we may spend more time worrying about our troubles than praying about them. And, we may spend more time fretting about our problems than solving them. A far better strategy, of course, is to pray as if everything depended entirely upon God and to work as if everything depended entirely upon us.

Life is an exercise in problem-solving. The question is not whether we will encounter problems; the real question is how we will choose to address them. When it comes to solving the problems of everyday living, we often know precisely what needs to be done, but we may be slow in doing it—especially if what needs to be done is difficult or uncomfortable for us. So we put off till tomorrow what should be done today.

The words of Psalm 34 remind us that the Lord solves problems for "people who do what is right." And usually, "doing what is right" means doing the uncomfortable work of confronting our problems sooner rather than later. So with no further ado, let the problem-solving begin . . . now!

Joy is the direct result of having God's perspective on our daily lives and the effect of loving our Lord enough to obey His commands and trust His promises.

Bill Bright

Values for Life

Keep Life In Perspective: Your life is an integral part of God's grand plan. So don't become unduly upset over the minor inconveniences of life, and don't worry too much about today's setbacks—they're temporary.

Timeless Wisdom for Godly Living

Instead of being frustrated and overwhelmed by all that is going on in our world, go to the Lord and ask Him to give you His eternal perspective.

Kay Arthur

Earthly fears are no fears at all. Answer the big question of eternity, and the little questions of life fall into perspective.

Max Lucado

*Since you have been raised to new life with Christ,
set your sights on the realities of heaven,
where Christ sits at God's right hand in the place
of honor and power.*

Colossians 3:1 NLT

The Bible is a remarkable commentary on perspective. Through its divine message, we are brought face to face with issues and tests in daily living and how, by the power of the Holy Spirit, we are enabled to respond positively to them.

Luci Swindoll

Live near to God, and so all things will appear to you little in comparison with eternal realities.

Robert Murray McCheyne

More Words from God's Word

Let us fix our eyes on Jesus, the author and perfecter of our faith, who for the joy set before him endured the cross, scorning its shame, and sat down at the right hand of the throne of God.

Hebrews 12:2 NIV

It's obvious, isn't it? The place where your treasure is, is the place you will most want to be, and end up being.

Luke 12:34 MSG

The thing you should want most is God's kingdom and doing what God wants. Then all these other things you need will be given to you.

Matthew 6:33 NCV

First pay attention to me, and then relax. Now you can take it easy— you're in good hands.

Proverbs 1:33 MSG

My Values for Life

When I encounter problems, I will tackle them sooner rather than later.

When I encounter problems, I will also look for solutions. I will not overestimate the size of my problems.

Check Your Value		
High	Med.	Low
___	___	___
___	___	___

God Is Perfect; We Are Not

*Those who wait for perfect weather will never plant seeds;
those who look at every cloud will never harvest crops . . . . Plant early in
the morning, and work until evening, because you don't know if this or
that will succeed. They might both do well.*

Ecclesiastes 11:4,6 NCV

You live in a world where expectations are high, incredibly high, or unreachable. The media delivers an endless stream of messages that tell you how to look, how to behave, how to eat, and how to dress. The media's expectations are impossible to meet—God's are not. God doesn't expect you to be perfect . . . and neither should you.

If you find yourself bound up by the chains of perfectionism, it's time to ask yourself whom you're trying to impress, and why. If you're trying to impress other people, it's time to reconsider your priorities.

Remember this: the expectations that really matter are not society's expectations or your friends' expectations. The expectations that matter are God's expectations, pure and simple. And everything else should take a back seat.

So do your best to please God, and don't worry too much about what other people think. And, when it comes to meeting the unrealistic expectations of our crazy world, forget about trying to meet those unrealistic expectations and concentrate, instead, on living a life that's pleasing to God.

God is not hard to please. He does not expect us to be absolutely perfect. He just expects us to keep moving toward Him and believing in Him, letting Him work with us to bring us into conformity to His will and ways.

Joyce Meyer

Values for Life

Accept Your Own Imperfections: If you're caught up in the modern-day push toward perfection, grow up . . . and then lighten up on yourself.

Timeless Wisdom for Godly Living

A perfectionist resists the truth that growing up in Christ is a process.

Susan Lenzkes

What makes a Christian a Christian is not perfection but forgiveness.

Max Lucado

We shall never come to the perfect man til we come to the perfect world.

Matthew Henry

Your beliefs about these things should be kept secret between you and God. People are happy if they can do what they think is right without feeling guilty.
Romans 14:22 NCV

The happiest people in the world are not those who have no problems, but the people who have learned to live with those things that are less than perfect.

James Dobson

God is so inconceivably good. He's not looking for perfection. He already saw it in Christ. He's looking for affection.

Beth Moore

More Words from God's Word

Let us lay aside every weight and the sin that so easily ensnares us, and run with endurance the race that lies before us, keeping our eyes on Jesus, the source and perfecter of our faith.

Hebrews 12:1-2 HCSB

My brethren, count it all joy when you fall into various trials, knowing that the testing of your faith produces patience. But let patience have its perfect work, that you may be perfect and complete, lacking nothing.

James 1:2-4 NKJV

And He said to me, "My grace is sufficient for you, for My strength is made perfect in weakness."

2 Corinthians 12:9 NKJV

My Values for Life

I am willing to accept the inevitable imperfections in other people.

I am willing to do my very best and leave the results up to God.

I think that it is important to acknowledge the difference between perfectionism and excellence.

Check Your Value		
High	Med.	Low
—	—	—
—	—	—
—	—	—

Trusting His Timetable

I trust in You, O LORD, I say, "You are my God."
My times are in Your hand.

Psalm 31:14-15 NASB

Are you a guy or girl in a hurry? If so, you're probably not the only one in your neighborhood. We human beings are, by our very nature, impatient. We are impatient with others, impatient with ourselves, and impatient with our Creator. We want things to happen according to our own timetables, but our Heavenly Father may have other plans. That's why we must learn the art of patience.

All too often we are unwilling to trust God's perfect timing. We allow ourselves to become apprehensive and anxious as we wait nervously for God to act. Usually, we know what we want, and we know precisely when we want it: right now, if not sooner. But, when God's plans differ from our own, we must train ourselves to trust in His infinite wisdom and in His infinite love.

As people living in a fast-paced world, many of us find that waiting quietly for God is quite troubling. But in our better moments, we realize that patience is not only a virtue, but it is also a commandment from the Creator.

Psalm 37:7 makes it clear that we should "Be still before the

Lord and wait patiently for Him" (NIV). But ours is a generation that usually places little value on stillness and patience. No matter. God instructs us to be patient in all things, and we must obey Him or suffer the consequences of His displeasure.

We must be patient with our families, with our friends, and with ourselves. We must also be patient with our Heavenly Father as He shapes our world (and our lives) in accordance with His timetable, not our own. And that's as it should be. After all, think how patient God has been with us.

> Waiting is an essential part of spiritual discipline.
> It can be the ultimate test of faith.
>
> *Anne Graham Lotz*

Values for Life

Trust God's Timing. God has very big plans in store for you, so trust Him and wait patiently for those plans to unfold. And remember: God's timing is best, so don't allow yourself to become discouraged if things don't work out exactly as you wish. Instead of worrying about your future, entrust it to God. He knows exactly what you need and exactly when you need it.

Timeless Wisdom for Godly Living

When there is perplexity there is always guidance—not always at the moment we ask, but in good time, which is God's time. There is no need to fret and stew.

Elisabeth Elliot

That time spent in waiting for a promise to be fulfilled is when faith envisions the outcome. It's in that gap that we can delight God. Without this kind of faith, it's impossible to please God (Hebrews 11:6).

Franklin Graham

Humble yourselves, therefore, under God's mighty hand, that he may lift you up in due time.
1 Peter 5:6 NIV

Even Jesus, clear as he was about his calling, had to get his instructions one day at a time. One time he was told to wait, another time to go.

Laurie Beth Jones

The stops of a good man are ordered by the Lord as well as his steps.

George Mueller

More Words from God's Word

From one man he made every nation of men, that they should inhabit the whole earth; and he determined the times set for them and the exact places where they should live.

Acts 17:26 NIV

He has made everything beautiful in its time. He has also set eternity in the hearts of men; yet they cannot fathom what God has done from beginning to end.

Ecclesiastes 3:11 NIV

He [Jesus] said to them: "It is not for you to know the times or dates the Father has set by his own authority."

Acts 1:7 NIV

My Values for Life

| Check Your Value | | |
| High | Med. | Low |

I take seriously the Bible's instructions to be patient.

I believe that patience is not idle waiting but that it is an activity that means being watchful as I wait for God to lead me.

Even when I don't understand the circumstances that confront me, I strive to wait patiently while serving the Lord.

Discovering His Peace

I leave you peace; my peace I give you.
I do not give it to you as the world does.
So don't let your hearts be troubled or afraid.

John 14:27 NCV

Oftentimes, our outer struggles are simply manifestations of the inner conflict that we feel when we stray from God's path.

Have you found the genuine peace that can be yours through Jesus Christ? Or are you still rushing after the illusion of "peace and happiness" that the world promises but cannot deliver? The beautiful words of John 14:27 remind us that Jesus offers us peace, not as the world gives, but as He alone gives: "Peace I leave with you. My peace I give to you. I do not give to you as the world gives. Your heart must not be troubled or fearful." Our challenge is to accept Christ's peace into our hearts and then, as best we can, to share His peace with our neighbors.

Today, as a gift to yourself, to your family, and to your friends, claim the inner peace that is your spiritual birthright: the peace of Jesus Christ. It is offered freely; it has been paid for in full; it is yours for the asking. So ask. And then share.

God's peace is like a river, not a pond.
In other words, a sense of health and
well-being, both of which are expressions of
the Hebrew shalom, can permeate our homes
even when we're in white-water rapids.

Beth Moore

Values for Life

Whatever It Is, God Can Handle It: Sometimes peace is a scarce commodity in a demanding, 21st-century world. How can we find the peace that we so desperately desire? By turning our days and our lives over to God. Elisabeth Elliot writes, "If my life is surrendered to God, all is well. Let me not grab it back, as though it were in peril in His hand but would be safer in mine!" May we give our lives, our hopes, and our prayers to the Father, and, by doing so, accept His will and His peace.

Timeless Wisdom for Godly Living

Believe and do what God says. The life-changing consequences will be limitless, and the results will be confidence and peace of mind.

Franklin Graham

We're prone to want God to change our circumstances, but He wants to change our character. We think that peace comes from the outside in, but it comes from the inside out.

Warren Wiersbe

If your sinful nature controls your mind, there is death. But if the Holy Spirit controls your mind, there is life and peace.

Romans 8:6 NLT

Thou hast formed us for Thyself, and our hearts are restless till they find rest in Thee.

St. Augustine

God has revealed to us a new reality that the world does not understand: In his eternal kingdom, what matters is being like our Father. That is the way to success and peace.

Mary Morrison Suggs

More Words from God's Word

Let us therefore follow after the things which make for peace, and things wherewith one may edify another.

Romans 14:19 KJV

And the peace of God, which surpasses all understanding, will guard your hearts and minds through Christ Jesus. Finally, brethren, whatever things are true, whatever things are noble, whatever things are just, whatever things are pure, whatever things are lovely, whatever things are of good report, if there is any virtue and if there is anything praiseworthy— meditate on these things.

Philippians 4:7-8 NKJV

I have told you these things, so that in me you may have peace. In this world you will have trouble. But take heart! I have overcome the world.

John 16:33 NIV

My Values for Life

I trust that God can give me a peace that passes my understanding.

I understand the importance of living a peaceful life.

I find that the more time I spend in prayer, the more peaceful I feel.

Check Your Value		
High	Med.	Low
—	—	—
—	—	—
—	—	—

Faith-filled Christian

Make me hear joy and gladness.

Psalm 51:8 NKJV

Face facts: pessimism and Christianity don't mix. Why? Because Christians have every reason to be optimistic about life here on earth and life eternal. Mrs. Charles E. Cowman advised, "Never yield to gloomy anticipation. Place your hope and confidence in God. He has no record of failure."

Sometimes, despite our trust in God, we may fall into the spiritual traps of worry, frustration, anxiety, or sheer exhaustion, and our hearts become heavy. What's needed is plenty of rest, a large dose of perspective, and God's healing touch, but not necessarily in that order.

Today, make this promise to yourself and keep it: vow to be a hope-filled Christian. Think optimistically about your life, your education, your family, and your future. Trust your hopes, not your fears. Take time to celebrate God's glorious creation. And then, when you've filled your heart with hope, share your optimism with others. They'll be better for it, and so will you. But not necessarily in that order.

Keep your feet on the ground,
but let your heart soar as high as it will.
Refuse to be average or to surrender to
the chill of your spiritual environment.

A. W. Tozer

Christ can put a spring in your step and
a thrill in your heart. Optimism and
cheerfulness are products of knowing Christ.

Billy Graham

Values for Life

Avoid Cynicism, Spread Optimism: Cynicism is contagious, and so is optimism. Choose your thoughts and your friends accordingly.

Timeless Wisdom for Godly Living

Hope looks for the good in people, opens doors for people, discovers what can be done to help, lights a candle, does not yield to cynicism. Hope sets people free.

Barbara Johnson

Make the least of all that goes and the most of all that comes. Don't regret what is past. Cherish what you have. Look forward to all that is to come. And most important of all, rely moment by moment on Jesus Christ.

Gigi Graham Tchividjian

I can do everything through him that gives me strength.
Philippians 4:13 NIV

We may run, walk, stumble, drive, or fly, but let us never lose sight of the reason for the journey, or miss a chance to see a rainbow on the way.

Gloria Gaither

Dark as my path may seem to others, I carry a magic light in my heart. Faith, the spiritual strong searchlight, illumines the way, and although sinister doubts lurk in the shadow, I walk unafraid toward the enchanted wood where the foliage is always green, where joy abides, where nightingales nest and sing, and where life and death are one in the presence of the Lord.

Helen Keller

More Words from God's Word

For God has not given us a spirit of fear, but of power and of love and of a sound mind.

2 Timothy 1:7 NLT

My cup runs over. Surely goodness and mercy shall follow me all the days of my life; and I will dwell in the house of the Lord Forever.

Psalm 23:5-6 NKJV

But if we look forward to something we don't have yet, we must wait patiently and confidently.

Romans 8:25 NLT

The Lord is my light and my salvation; whom shall I fear? The Lord is the strength of my life; of whom shall I be afraid?

Psalm 27:1 KJV

My Values for Life

	Check Your Value	
High	Med.	Low

I understand the importance of counting my blessings, not my hardships.

I will look for opportunities, not obstructions; and I will look for possibilities, not problems.

I understand the need to associate with people who encourage me to be optimistic, upbeat, and cheerful.

Behaviors That Are Pleasing to Whom?

Do you think I am trying to make people accept me?
No, God is the One I am trying to please. Am I trying to please people?
If I still wanted to please people, I would not be a servant of Christ.

Galatians 1:10 NCV

Whom will you try to please today: God or man? Your primary obligation, of course, is to please your Father in heaven, not your friends in the neighborhood. But even if you're a devoted Christian, you may, from time to time, feel the urge to impress your peers—and sometimes that urge can be strong.

Peer pressure can be a good thing or a bad thing, depending upon your peers. If your peers encourage you to follow God's will and to obey His commandments, then you'll experience positive peer pressure, and that's good. But, if you are involved with friends who encourage you to do foolish things, you're facing a different kind of peer pressure . . . and you'd better beware. When you feel pressured to do things—or to say things—that lead you away from God, you're aiming straight for trouble. So don't do the "easy" thing or the "popular" thing. Do the right thing, and don't worry about winning popularity contests.

Here are a few things to remember about peer pressure:

1. Peer pressure exists, and you will experience it.
2. If your peers encourage you to behave yourself, to honor God, and to become a better person, peer pressure can actually be a good thing . . . up to a point. But remember: you don't have to be perfect to be wonderful. So if you're trying to be perfect, lighten up on yourself, and while you're at it, lighten up on others, too.
3. If your friends are encouraging you to misbehave or underachieve, find new friends. Today.

Rick Warren correctly observed, "Those who follow the crowd usually get lost in it." Are you satisfied to follow that crowd? If so, you will probably pay a heavy price for your shortsightedness. But if you're determined to follow the One from Galilee, He will guide your steps and bless your undertakings. To sum it up, here's your choice: you can choose to please God first, or you can fall prey to peer pressure. The choice is yours—and so are the consequences.

> Comparison is the root of all feelings of inferiority.
>
> *James Dobson*

Values for Life

Put Peer Pressure to Work for You: How? By associating with people who, by their actions and their words, will encourage you to become a better person.

Timeless Wisdom for Godly Living

There is nothing that makes more cowards and feeble men than public opinion.

Henry Ward Beecher

When we are set free from the bondage of pleasing others, when we are free from currying others' favor and others' approval—then no one will be able to make us miserable or dissatisfied. And then, if we know we have pleased God, contentment will be our consolation.

Kay Arthur

He who walks with the wise grows wise,
but a companion of fools suffers harm.
Proverbs 13:20 NIV

It is comfortable to know that we are responsible to God and not to man. It is a small matter to be judged of man's judgement.

Lottie Moon

You will get untold flak for prioritizing God's revealed and present will for your life over man's . . . but, boy, is it worth it.

Beth Moore

If you try to be everything to everybody, you will end up being nothing to anybody.

Vance Havner

More Words from God's Word

Therefore, whether we are at home or away, we make it our aim to be pleasing to Him. For we must all appear before the judgment seat of Christ, so that each may be repaid for what he has done in the body, whether good or bad.

2 Corinthians 5:9-10 HCSB

May the words of my mouth and the thoughts of my heart be pleasing to you, O Lord, my rock and my redeemer.

Psalm 19:14 NLT

Do not conform any longer to the pattern of this world, but be transformed by the renewing of your mind. Then you will be able to test and approve what God's will is—his good, pleasing and perfect will.

Romans 12:2 NIV

My Values for Life

	Check Your Value	
High	Med.	Low

I understand the importance of pleasing God first.

___ ___ ___

I actively seek out wise friends who help me make right choices.

___ ___ ___

I understand that being obedient to God means that I cannot always please other people.

___ ___ ___

Opportunities Everywhere

Therefore, as we have opportunity, we must work for the good of all, especially for those who belong to the household of faith.

Galatians 6:10 HCSB

s you look at the landscape of your life, do you see opportunities, possibilities, and blessings, or do you focus, instead, upon the more negative scenery? Do you spend more time counting your blessings or your misfortunes? If you've acquired the unfortunate habit of focusing too intently upon the negative aspects of life, then your spiritual vision is in need of correction.

Whether you realize it or not, opportunities are whirling around you like stars crossing the night sky: beautiful to observe, but too numerous to count. Yet you may be too concerned with the challenges of everyday living to notice those opportunities. That's why you should slow down occasionally, catch your breath, and focus your thoughts on two things: the talents God has given you and the opportunities that He has placed before you. God is leading you in the direction of those opportunities. Your task is to watch carefully, to pray fervently, and to act accordingly.

Are you willing to place your future in the hands of a loving and all-knowing God? Do you trust in the ultimate goodness of His plan for your life? Will you face today's challenges with optimism and hope? You should. After all, God created you for a very important purpose: His purpose. And you still have important work to do: His work. And the time to start doing that work is now.

Life is a glorious opportunity.

Billy Graham

Values for Life

Familiarize Yourself with the Opportunities of Tomorrow: The world of tomorrow is filled with opportunities for those who are willing to find them and work for them. Make certain that you have more than a passing familiarity with the-ever shifting sands of our changing America.

Timeless Wisdom for Godly Living

We are all faced with a series of great opportunities, brilliantly disguised as unsolvable problems. Unsolvable without God's wisdom, that is.

Charles Swindoll

Don't waste today's time cluttering up tomorrow's opportunities with yesterday's troubles.

Barbara Johnson

Make the most of every opportunity.
Colossians 4:5 NIV

Every day we live is a priceless gift of God, loaded with possibilities to learn something new, to gain fresh insights.

Dale Evans Rogers

Lovely, complicated wrappings; sheath the gift of one-day-more; breathless, I untie the package—never lived this day before!

Gloria Gaither

With the right attitude and a willingness to pay the price, almost anyone can pursue nearly any opportunity and achieve it.

John Maxwell

More Words from God's Word

Let us not lose heart in doing good, for in due time we shall reap if we do not grow weary. So then, while we have opportunity, let us do good to all men, and especially to those who are of the household of the faith.

Galatians 6:9-10 NASB

Dear brothers and sisters, whenever trouble comes your way, let it be an opportunity for joy. For when your faith is tested, your endurance has a chance to grow. So let it grow, for when your endurance is fully developed, you will be strong in character and ready for anything.

James 1:2-4 NLT

Jesus was matter-of-fact: "Embrace this God-life. Really embrace it, and nothing will be too much for you.

Mark 11:22-23 MSG

If God be for us, who can be against us?

Romans 8:31 KJV

My Values for Life

I trust that God has important things for me to do.

I understand the importance of looking for opportunities, not stumbling blocks.

I understand that life is brief, and I will strive to make the most of my time here on earth.

Check Your Value		
High	Med.	Low
—	—	—
—	—	—
—	—	—

An Obedient Heart

Anyone who listens to my teaching and obeys me is wise,
like a person who builds a house on solid rock. Though the rain comes in
torrents and the floodwaters rise and the winds beat against that house,
it won't collapse, because it is built on rock.

Matthew 7:24-25 NLT

O bedience to God is determined, not by words, but by deeds. Talking about righteousness is easy; living righteously is far more difficult, especially in today's temptation-filled world.

Since God created Adam and Eve, we human beings have been rebelling against our Creator. Why? Because we are unwilling to trust God's Word, and we are unwilling to follow His commandments. God has given us a guidebook for righteous living called the Holy Bible. It contains thorough instructions which, if followed, lead to fulfillment, abundance, and salvation. But, if we choose to ignore God's commandments, the results are as predictable as they are tragic.

In Ephesians 2:10 we read, "For we are His workmanship, created in Christ Jesus for good works" (NKJV). These words are instructive: We are not saved by good works, but for good works. Good works are not the root, but rather the fruit of our salvation.

When we seek righteousness in our own lives—and when we seek the companionship of those who do likewise—we reap the spiritual rewards that God intends for our lives. When we behave ourselves as godly men and women, we honor God. When we live righteously and according to God's commandments, He blesses us in ways that we cannot fully understand.

Do you seek God's peace and His blessings? Then obey Him. When you're faced with a difficult choice or a powerful temptation, seek God's counsel and trust the counsel He gives. Invite God into your heart and live according to His commandments. When you do, you will be blessed today and tomorrow and forever.

> God's promises aren't celestial life preservers that He throws out to strangers in the storm. They are expressions of His love and care, given to His children who walk with Him and seek to obey Him.
>
> *Warren Wiersbe*

Values for Life

Obedience leads to spiritual growth: Anne Graham Lotz correctly observed, "If you want to discover your spiritual gifts, start obeying God. As you serve Him, you will find that He has given you the gifts that are necessary to follow through in obedience."

Timeless Wisdom for Godly Living

What our Lord said about cross-bearing and obedience is not in fine type. It is in bold print on the face of the contract.

Vance Havner

God asked both Noah and Joshua to do something unusual and difficult. They did it, and their obedience brought them deliverance.

Mary Morrison Suggs

Likewise you younger people,
submit yourselves to your elders.
1 Peter 5:5 NKJV

Rejoicing is a matter of obedience to God—an obedience that will start you on the road to peace and contentment.

Kay Arthur

God's love for His children is unconditional, no strings attached. But, God's blessings on our lives do come with a condition—obedience. If we are to receive the fullness of God's blessings, we must obey Him and keep His commandments.

Jim Gallery

Obedience is the outward expression of your love of God.

Henry Blackaby

More Words from God's Word

Blessed is every one who fears the Lord, who walks in His ways.

Psalm 128:1 NKJV

Teach me, O LORD, to follow your decrees; then I will keep them to the end. Give me understanding, and I will keep your law and obey it with all my heart.

Psalm 119:33-34 NIV

Not everyone who says to me, "Lord, Lord," will enter the kingdom of heaven, but only he who does the will of my Father who is in heaven.

Matthew 7:21 NIV

For God is working in you, giving you the desire to obey him and the power to do what pleases him.

Philippians 2:13 NLT

My Values for Life

I understand that my obedience to God is a demonstration of the gratitude that I feel in my heart for the blessings I have been given.

When I obey God, I feel better about myself.

Obedience to God may not always be easy or pleasant, but it is always satisfying.

Check Your Value		
High	Med.	Low
—	—	—
—	—	—
—	—	—

Really Living Means Really Loving

Love one another deeply, from the heart.

1 Peter 1:22 NIV

ove, like everything else in this wonderful world, begins and ends with God, but the middle part belongs to us. During the brief time that we have here on earth, God has given each of us the opportunity to become a loving person—or not. God has given each of us the opportunity to be kind, to be courteous, to be cooperative, and to be forgiving—or not. God has given each of us the chance to obey the Golden Rule, or to make up our own rules as we go. If we obey God's rules, we're safe, but if we do otherwise, we're headed for trouble in a hurry.

There's an old saying that's both familiar and true: If you aren't loving, you aren't living. But here in the real world, it isn't always easy to love other people, especially when those people have done things to hurt you. Still, God's Word is clear: you are instructed to love others despite their imperfections.

The Christian path is an exercise in love and forgiveness. If you are to walk in Christ's footsteps, you must forgive those who have done you harm, and you must accept Christ's love by sharing it freely with family, friends, neighbors, and even strangers.

God does not intend for you to experience mediocre relationships; He created you for far greater things. Building lasting relationships requires compassion, wisdom, empathy, kindness, courtesy, and forgiveness. If that sounds like work, it is—which is perfectly fine with God. Why? Because He knows that you are capable of doing that work, and because He knows that the fruits of your labors will enrich the lives of your loved ones and the lives of generations yet unborn.

Love seeks one thing only: the good of the one loved. It leaves all the other secondary effects to take care of themselves. Love, therefore, is its own reward.

Thomas Merton

Values for Life

Since you love them, say so! Since you sincerely love your family and friends, make sure that you tell them so . . . a lot!

Timeless Wisdom for Godly Living

We have the Lord, but He Himself has recognized that we need the touch of a human hand. He Himself came down and lived among us as a man. We cannot see Him now, but blessed be the tie that binds human hearts in Christian love.

Vance Havner

The Christian life has two different dimensions: faith toward God and love toward men. You cannot separate the two.

Warren Wiersbe

Listening is loving.

Zig Ziglar

And the Lord make you to increase and abound in love one toward another, and toward all men.
1 Thessalonians 3:12 KJV

To love another person is to see the face of God.

Victor Hugo

Love is an attribute of God. To love others is evidence of a genuine faith.

Kay Arthur

More Words from God's Word

Love

Though I speak with the tongues of men and of angels, but have not love, I have become sounding brass or a clanging cymbal. And though I have the gift of prophecy, and understand all mysteries and all knowledge, and though I have all faith, so that I could remove mountains, but have not love, I am nothing. And though I bestow all my goods to feed the poor, and though I give my body to be burned, but have not love, it profits me nothing. Love suffers long and is kind; love does not envy; love does not parade itself, is not puffed up; does not behave rudely, does not seek its own, is not provoked, thinks no evil; does not rejoice in iniquity, but rejoices in the truth; bears all things, believes all things, hopes all things, endures all things. Love never fails . . . . And now abide faith, hope, love, these three; but the greatest of these is love.

1 Corinthians 13:1-8, 13 NKJV

My Values for Life

As a follower of Christ, I understand that I am commanded to love other people, and I take that commandment seriously.

Because I place a high priority on my relationships, I am willing to invest the time and energy that are required to make those relationships work.

When I have been hurt by someone, I understand the importance of forgiving that person as quickly as possible and as completely as possible.

Check Your Value		
High	Med.	Low
—	—	—
—	—	—
—	—	—

The Courage to Dream

But as for me, I will always have hope; I will praise you more and more.

Psalm 71:14 NIV

Are you willing to entertain the possibility that God has big plans in store for you? Hopefully so. Yet sometimes, especially if you've recently experienced a life-altering disappointment, you may find it difficult to envision a brighter future for yourself and your family. If so, it's time to reconsider your own capabilities . . . and God's.

Your Heavenly Father created you with unique gifts and untapped talents; your job is to tap them. When you do, you'll begin to feel an increasing sense of confidence in yourself and in your future. As the old saying goes, if you feed your faith, your doubts will starve to death.

On occasion, you will face the inevitable disappointments of life. And sometimes, you must endure life-altering personal losses that leave you breathless. On such occasions, you may be tempted to abandon your dreams. Don't do it! Instead, trust that God is preparing you for greater things.

Concentration camp survivor Corrie ten Boom observed, "Every experience God gives us, every person he brings into our lives, is the perfect preparation for the future that only he can see." These words apply to you.

Are you excited about the opportunities of today and thrilled by the possibilities of tomorrow? Do you confidently expect God to lead you to a place of abundance, peace, and joy? And, when your days on earth are over, do you expect to receive the priceless gift of eternal life? If you trust God's promises, and if you have welcomed God's Son into your heart, then you believe that your future is intensely and eternally bright.

It takes courage to dream big dreams. You will discover that courage when you do three things: accept the past, trust God to handle the future, and make the most of the time He has given you today.

Nothing is too difficult for God, and no dreams are too big for Him—not even yours. So start living—and dreaming—accordingly.

Dreaming the dream of God is not for cowards.

Joey Johnson

Values for Life

Making your dreams come true requires work. John Maxwell writes, "The gap between your vision and your present reality can only be filled through a commitment to maximize your potential." Enough said.

Timeless Wisdom for Godly Living

Always stay connected to people and seek out things that bring you joy. Dream with abandon. Pray confidently.

Barbara Johnson

Sometimes our dreams were so big that it took two people to dream them.

Marie T. Freeman

We must be willing to give up every dream but God's dream.

Larry Crabb

May he grant your heart's desire and fulfill all your plans.
Psalm 20:4 NLT

The future lies all before us. Shall it only be a slight advance upon what we usually do? Ought it not to be a bound, a leap forward to altitudes of endeavor and success undreamed of before?

Annie Armstrong

To make your dream come true, you have to stay awake.

Dennis Swanberg

More Words from God's Word

I came so they can have real and eternal life, more and better life than they ever dreamed of.

John 10:10 MSG

May He grant you according to your heart's desire, and fulfill all your purpose.

Psalm 20:4 NKJV

Trust in the LORD *with all your heart; do not depend on your own understanding.*

Proverbs 3:5 NLT

For with God nothing will be impossible.

Luke 1:37 NKJV

My Values for Life

	Check Your Value	
High	Med.	Low

I prayerfully seek to understand God's plans for my life.

I work to know God's plan for my life, and I work to fulfill that plan.

I try not to place limitations on myself, and I refuse to place limitations on God's power to use me for His purposes.

Dreams

Beyond Loneliness

I am not alone, because the Father is with Me.

John 16:32 NKJV

I f you're like most people, you've experienced occasional bouts of loneliness. If so, you understand the genuine pain that accompanies those feelings that "nobody cares." In truth, lots of people care about you, but at times, you may hardly notice their presence.

Sometimes, intense feelings of loneliness may be the result of depression (if you think this might be the case, talk things over with your family, with your pastor, and with your physician). Other times, however, your feelings of loneliness come as a result of your own hesitation, the hesitation to "get out there and make new friends."

Why do so many of us hesitate to meet new people and make new friends? Several reasons: some of us are just plain shy, and because of our shyness, we find it more difficult to interact with unfamiliar people. Others, while not exceedingly shy, are overly attuned to the potential of rejection). Still others may be so self-critical that they feel unworthy of the attentions of others.

In truth, the world is literally teeming with people who are looking for new friends. And yet, ironically enough, too many of us allow our friendships to wither away, not because we intentionally alienate others, but because we simply don't pay enough attention to them.

The philosopher William James observed, "Human beings are born into this little span of life, and among the best things that life has to offer are its friendships and intimacies. Yet, humans leave their friendships with no cultivation, letting them grow as they will by the roadside." James understood that when we leave our friendships unattended, the resulting harvest is predictably slim. Don't let it happen to you!

Loneliness is the first thing which God's eye named as not good.

John Milton

Values for Life

Want to meet more people? Become more involved in your church or in community service: they'll welcome your participation, and you'll welcome the chance to connect with more and more people.

Timeless Wisdom for Godly Living

When we are living apart for God, we can be lonely and lost, even in the midst of a crowd.

Billy Graham

We are born helpless. As soon as we are fully conscious we discover loneliness. We need others physically, emotionally, intellectually; we need them if we are to know anything, even ourselves.

C. S. Lewis

> *A friend loves you all the time,*
> *and a brother helps in time of trouble.*
> Proverbs 17:17 NCV

Are you feeling lonely today because of suffering? My word to you is simply this: Jesus Christ is there with you.

Warren Wiersbe

God accompanies his children into exile. No space is devoid of God. God is everywhere, even in suffering and in the very heart of punishment. What happens to us touches God. What happens to him concerns us.

Elie Wiesel

More Words from God's Word

I am not alone, because the Father is with Me.

John 16:32 NKJV

Do not be afraid or discouraged. For the LORD your God is with you wherever you go.

Joshua 1:9 NLT

Jacob said, "For what a relief it is to see your friendly smile. It is like seeing the smile of God!"

Genesis 33:10 NLT

Fear not, for I am with you; Be not dismayed, for I am your God. I will strengthen you.

Isaiah 41:10 NKJV

My Values for Life

	Check Your Value	
High	Med.	Low

When I feel lonely, I understand that the feeling is temporary.

— — —

I understand that making friends—and keeping friends— often requires effort on my part.

— — —

I know that I am never alone because God is always near.

— — —

Life with a Capital L

I came so they can have real and eternal life,
more and better life than they ever dreamed of.

John 10:10 MSG

Life can be tough sometimes, but it's also wonderful—and it's a glorious gift from God. How will you use that gift? Will you treat this day as a precious treasure from your Heavenly Father, or will you take the next 24 hours for granted? The answer should be obvious: Every day, including this one, comes gift-wrapped from God—your job is to unwrap that gift, to use it wisely, and to give thanks to the Giver.

Instead of sleepwalking through life, you must wake up and live in the precious present. Each waking moment holds the potential to celebrate, to serve, to share, or to love. Because you are a person with incalculable potential, each moment has incalculable value. Your challenge is to experience each day to the full as you seek to live in accordance with God's plan for your life. When you do, you'll experience His abundance and His peace.

Are you willing to treat this day (and every one hereafter) as a special gift to be savored and celebrated? You should—and if you seek to Live with a capital L, you most certainly will.

The measure of a life, after all, is not its duration but its donation.

Corrie ten Boom

Jesus wants Life for us,
Life with a capital L.

John Eldredge

Values for Life

Be a Realistic Optimist About Life: Your attitude toward the future will help create your future. You might as well put the self-fulfilling prophecy to work for you, and besides, life is far too short to be a pessimist.

Timeless Wisdom for Godly Living

When we invite Jesus into our lives, we experience life in the fullest, most vital sense.

Catherine Marshall

You've heard the saying, "Life is what you make it." That means we have a choice. We can choose to have a life full of frustration and fear, but we can just as easily choose one of joy and contentment.

Dennis Swanberg

> *I am the way and the truth and the life.*
> *No one comes to the Father except through me.*
> John 14:6 NIV

The world has never been stable. Jesus Himself was born into the cruelest and most unstable of worlds. No, we have babies and keep trusting and living because the Resurrection is true! The Resurrection was not just a one-time event in history; it is a principle built into the very fabric of our beings, a fact reverberating from every cell of creation: Life wins! Life wins!

Gloria Gaither

I don't know about you, but I want to do more than survive life . . . . I want to mount up like the eagle and glide over rocky crags, nest in the tallest of trees, dive for nourishment in the deepest of mountain lakes, and soar on the wings of the wind.

Barbara Johnson

More Words from God's Word

Then Jesus said to his disciples, "If anyone would come after me, he must deny himself and take up his cross and follow me. For whoever wants to save his life will lose it, but whoever loses his life for me will find it."

Matthew 16:24-25 NIV

For to me to live is Christ, and to die is gain.

Philippians 1:21 KJV

He who pursues righteousness and love finds life, prosperity and honor.

Proverbs 21:21 NIV

God chose you to be his people, so I urge you now to live the life to which God called you.

Ephesians 4:1 NKJV

My Values for Life

I consider my life to be a priceless gift from God.

I understand the importance of spending time each day thanking God for his blessings.

I slow down to marvel at the beauty of God's glorious creation.

I strive to make every day a cause for celebration.

Check Your Value		
High	Med.	Low
—	—	—
—	—	—
—	—	—
—	—	—

Valuing God's Guidance

In all your ways acknowledge Him, and He shall direct your paths.

Proverbs 3:6 NKJV

When we genuinely seek to know God's will—when we prayerfully seek His wisdom and His guidance—our Heavenly Father carefully leads us over the peaks and valleys of life. And, as Christians, we can be comforted: Whether we find ourselves at the pinnacle of the mountain or the darkest depths of the valley, God is always there with us.

C. S. Lewis observed, "I don't doubt that the Holy Spirit guides your decisions from within when you make them with the intention of pleasing God. The error would be to think that He speaks only within, whereas in reality He speaks also through Scripture, the Church, Christian friends, and books." These words remind us that God has many ways to make Himself known. Our challenge is to make ourselves open to His instruction.

Do you place a high value on God's guidance, and do you talk to Him regularly about matters great and small? Or do you talk with God on a haphazard basis? If you're wise, you'll form the habit of speaking to God early and often. But you won't stop there—you'll also study God's Word, you'll obey God's commandments, and you'll associate with people who do likewise.

So, if you're unsure of your next step, lean upon God's promises and lift your prayers to Him. Remember that God is always near—always trying to get His message through. Open yourself to Him every day, and trust Him to guide your path. When you do, you'll be protected today, tomorrow, and forever.

A spiritual discipline is necessary in order to move slowly from an absurd to an obedient life, from a life filled with noisy worries to a life in which there is some free inner space where we can listen to our God and follow his guidance.

Henri Nouwen

Values for Life

Need guidance? Pray for it. When you seek it, He will give it.

Timeless Wisdom for Godly Living

God will prove to you how good and acceptable and perfect His will is when He's got His hands on the steering wheel of your life.

Stuart & Jill Briscoe

The Bible is not a guidebook to a theological museum. It is a road map showing us the way into neglected or even forgotten glories of the living God.

Raymond Ortlund

Men give advice; God gives guidance.

Leonard Ravenhill

> *I will instruct you and teach you in the way you should go; I will guide you with My eye.*
>
> Psalm 32:8 NKJV

It's a bit like river rafting with an experienced guide. You may begin to panic when the guide steers you straight into a steep waterfall, especially if another course appears much safer. Yet, after you've emerged from the swirling depths and wiped the spray from your eyes, you see that just beyond the seemingly "safe" route was a series of jagged rocks. Your guide knew what he was doing after all.

Shirley Dobson

More Words from God's Word

The true children of God are those who let God's Spirit lead them.

Romans 8:14 NCV

In thee, O Lord, do I put my trust; let me never be put into confusion.

Psalm 71:1 KJV

Our God forever and ever . . . will guide us until death.

Psalm 48:14 NASB

Every morning he wakes me. He teaches me to listen like a student. The Lord God helps me learn . . . .

Isaiah 50:4-5 NCV

Teach me Your way, O LORD, and lead me in a level path.

Psalm 27:11 NASB

My Values for Life

I understand the importance of seeking God's wisdom and His guidance.

I allow God to guide me by His Word and by His Spirit.

I understand that whenever I genuinely trust God to guide my path, I will be comforted.

Check Your Value		
High	Med.	Low
—	—	—
—	—	—
—	—	—

The Choice to Rejoice

Always be full of joy in the Lord. I say it again—rejoice!

Philippians 4:4 NLT

Have you made the choice to rejoice? If you're a Christian, you have every reason to be joyful. After all, the ultimate battle has already been won on the cross at Calvary. And if your life has been transformed by Christ's sacrifice, then you, as a recipient of God's grace, have every reason to live joyfully. Yet sometimes, amid the inevitable hustle and bustle of life here on earth, you may lose sight of your blessings as you wrestle with the challenges of everyday life.

Do you want to be a happy, contented Christian? If so, here are some things you should do: Love God and His Son; depend upon God for strength; try, to the best of your abilities, to follow God's will; and strive to obey His Holy Word. When you do these things, you'll discover that happiness goes hand-in-hand with righteousness. The happiest people are not those who rebel against God; the happiest people are those who love God and obey His commandments.

What does life have in store for you? A world full of possibilities (of course it's up to you to seize them), and God's promise of abundance (of course it's up to you to accept it). So, as you embark upon the next phase of your journey, remember to celebrate the life that God has given you. Your Creator has blessed you beyond measure. Honor Him with your prayers, your words, your deeds, and your joy.

Finding joy means first of all finding Jesus.

Jill Briscoe

The Christian lifestyle is not one of legalistic do's and don'ts, but one that is positive, attractive, and joyful.

Vonette Bright

Values for Life

Joy begins with a choice—the choice to establish a genuine relationship with God and His Son. As Amy Carmichael correctly observed, "Joy is not gush; joy is not mere jolliness. Joy is perfect acquiescence, acceptance, and rest in God's will, whatever comes."

Timeless Wisdom for Godly Living

Christ is not only a remedy for your weariness and trouble, but he will give you an abundance of the contrary: joy and delight. They who come to Christ do not only come to a resting-place after they have been wandering in a wilderness, but they come to a banqueting-house where they may rest, and where they may feast. They may cease from their former troubles and toils, and they may enter upon a course of delights and spiritual joys.

Jonathan Edwards

Rejoice, and be exceeding glad:
for great is your reward in heaven . . . .
Matthew 5:12 KJV

Joy is the great note all throughout the Bible.

Oswald Chambers

Let God have you, and let God love you—and don't be surprised if your heart begins to hear music you've never heard and your feet learn to dance as never before.

Max Lucado

More Words from God's Word

Let the hearts of those who seek the Lord rejoice. Look to the Lord and his strength; seek his face always.

1 Chronicles 16:10-11 NIV

The Word of Life appeared right before our eyes; we saw it happen! And now we're telling you in most sober prose that what we witnessed was, incredibly, this: The infinite Life of God himself took shape before us. We saw it, we heard it, and now we're telling you so you can experience it along with us, this experience of communion with the Father and his Son, Jesus Christ. Our motive for writing is simply this: We want you to enjoy this, too. Your joy will double our joy!

1 John 1:2-4 MSG

Shout with joy to the LORD, O earth! Worship the LORD with gladness. Come before him, singing with joy.

Psalm 100:1-2 NLT

My Values for Life

I do my best to treat each day of my life as a cause for celebration.

I praise God many times each day.

I do what I can to share my enthusiasm with family, with friends, and with the world.

Check Your Value		
High	Med.	Low
—	—	—
—	—	—
—	—	—

Hope Now!

You are my hope; O Lord GOD, You are my confidence.

Psalm 71:5 NASB

There are few sadder sights on earth than the sight of a girl or guy who has lost hope. In difficult times, hope can be elusive, but those who place their faith in God's promises need never lose it. After all, God is good; His love endures; He has promised His children the gift of eternal life. And, God keeps His promises.

Despite God's promises, despite Christ's love, and despite our countless blessings, we're only human, and we can still lose hope from time to time. When we do, we need the encouragement of Christian friends, the life-changing power of prayer, and the healing truth of God's Holy Word.

If you find yourself falling into the spiritual traps of worry and discouragement, seek the healing touch of Jesus and the encouraging words of fellow believers. And if you find a friend in need, remind him or her of the peace that is found through a genuine relationship with Christ. It was Christ who promised, "I have told you these things so that in Me you may have peace. In the world you have suffering. But take courage! I have conquered the world" (John 16: 33 HCSB). This world can be a place of trials and troubles, but as believers, we are secure. God has promised us peace, joy, and eternal life. And, of course, God keeps His promises today, tomorrow, and forever.

When you say a situation or a person is
hopeless, you are slamming the door
in the face of God.

Charles L. Allen

Faith looks back and draws courage;
hope looks ahead and keeps desire alive.

John Eldredge

Values for Life

Never be afraid to hope—or to ask—for a miracle.

Timeless Wisdom for Godly Living

Live for today, but hold your hands open to tomorrow. Anticipate the future and its changes with joy. There is a seed of God's love in every event, every circumstance, every unpleasant situation in which you may find yourself.

Barbara Johnson

Nothing in this world is more fundamental for success in life than hope, and this star pointed to our only source of true hope: Jesus Christ.

D. James Kennedy

Be joyful in hope, patient in affliction, faithful in prayer.
Romans 12:12 NIV

When you and I are related to Jesus Christ, our strength and wisdom and peace and joy and love and hope may run out, but His life rushes in to keep us filled to the brim. We are showered with blessings, not because of anything we have or have not done, but simply because of Him.

Anne Graham Lotz

No other religion, no other philosophy promises new bodies, hearts, and minds. Only in the Gospel of Christ do hurting people find such incredible hope.

Joni Eareckson Tada

More Words from God's Word

I find rest in God; only he gives me hope.

Psalm 62:5 NCV

Relax, everything's going to be all right; rest, everything's coming together; open your hearts, love is on the way!

Jude 1:2 MSG

Full of hope, you'll relax, confident again; you'll look around, sit back, and take it easy.

Job 11:18 MSG

For I know the thoughts that I think toward you, says the Lord, thoughts of peace and not of evil, to give you a future and a hope. Then you will call upon Me and go and pray to Me, and I will listen to you.

Jeremiah 29:11-12 NKJV

My Values for Life

I believe that genuine hope begins with hope in a sovereign God.

I understand that action is an antidote to worry.

I believe that God offers me "a peace that passes understanding," and I desire to accept God's peace.

Check Your Value		
High	Med.	Low
—	—	—
—	—	—
—	—	—

Valuing God's Word

Thy word is a lamp unto my feet, and a light unto my path.

Psalm 119:105 KJV

Too many Christians treat the Bible like any other book. But get this loud and clear: THE BIBLE ISN'T LIKE ANY OTHER BOOK! Period! And if you're wise, you'll give your Bible the reverence and the attention that it deserves.

Is God's Word a bright spotlight that guides your path, or is it a tiny nightlight that occasionally flickers? Is God's Word your indispensable compass for everyday living, or is it relegated to Sunday morning services? Do you read the Bible faithfully or sporadically? The answer to these questions will determine the direction of your thoughts, the direction of your day, and the direction of your life.

George Mueller observed, "The vigor of our spiritual lives will be in exact proportion to the place held by the Bible in our lives and in our thoughts." Think of it like this: the more you use your Bible, the more God will use you.

God's Word can be a roadmap to a place of righteousness and abundance. Make it your roadmap. God's wisdom can be a light to guide your steps. Claim it as your light today, tomorrow, and every day of your life—and then walk confidently in the footsteps of God's only begotten Son.

God has given us all sorts of counsel
and direction in his written Word; thank God,
we have it written down in black and white.

John Eldredge

Prayer and the Word are inseparably
linked together. Power in the use of either
depends on the presence of the other.

Andrew Murray

Values for Life

Trust God's Word: Charles Swindoll writes, "There are four words
I wish we would never forget, and they are, 'God keeps his word.'"
And remember this: When it comes to studying God's Word, school is
always in session.

Timeless Wisdom for Godly Living

God can see clearly no matter how dark or foggy the night is. Trust His Word to guide you safely home.

Lisa Whelchel

One of the greatest ways God changes me is by bringing Scripture to mind that I have hidden deep in my heart. And, He always picks the right Scripture at the right time.

Evelyn Christianson

All Scripture is given by inspiration of God, and is profitable for doctrine, for reproof, for correction, for instruction in righteousness.

2 Timothy 3:16 KJV

It takes calm, thoughtful, prayerful meditation on the Word to extract its deepest nourishment.

Vance Havner

The promises of Scripture are not mere pious hopes or sanctified guesses. They are more than sentimental words to be printed on decorated cards for Sunday School children. They are eternal verities. They are true. There is no perhaps about them.

Peter Marshall

More Words from God's Word

For the word of God is living and effective and sharper than any two-edged sword, penetrating as far as to divide soul, spirit, joints, and marrow; it is a judge of the ideas and thoughts of the heart.

Hebrews 4:12 HCSB

Heaven and earth will pass away, but my words will never pass away.

Matthew 24:35 NIV

Man shall not live by bread alone, but by every word that proceeds from the mouth of God.

Matthew 4:4 NKJV

So then faith comes by hearing, and hearing by the word of God.

Romans 10:17 NKJV

My Values for Life

I value the Bible as God's Word, and I believe that the Bible is true.

When my behavior is inconsistent with God's Word, I understand the need to change my behavior.

I have a regular time when I study the Bible and meditate upon its meaning for my life.

Check Your Value		
High	Med.	Low
—	—	—
—	—	—
—	—	—

The Bible

Good Samaritan 101

Each one of us needs to look after the good of the people around us,
asking ourselves, "How can I help?" That's exactly what Jesus did.
He didn't make it easy for himself by avoiding people's troubles,
but waded right in and helped out. "I took on the troubles of the troubled,"
is the way Scripture puts it.

Romans 15:2-3 MSG

Sometimes we would like to help make the world a better place, but we're not sure of the best way to do it. Jesus told the story of the "Good Samaritan," a man who helped a fellow traveler when no one else would. We, too, should be good Samaritans when we encounter people who need our help.

The words of Jesus are unambiguous: "Freely you have received, freely give" (Matthew 10:8 NIV). As followers of Christ, we are commanded to be generous with our friends, with our families, and with those in need. We must give freely of our time, our possessions, and, most especially, our love.

In 2 Corinthians 9, Paul reminds us that when we sow the seeds of generosity, we reap bountiful rewards in accordance with God's plan for our lives: "Now this I say, he who sows sparingly will also reap sparingly, and he who sows bountifully will also reap bountifully. Each one must do just as he has purposed in his heart,

not grudgingly or under compulsion, for God loves a cheerful giver"
(vv. 6-7 NASB).

Today, take God's words to heart and make this pledge:
Wherever you happen to be, be a good Samaritan. Somebody near
you needs your assistance, and you need the spiritual rewards that
will be yours when you lend a helping hand.

We can never untangle all the woes in other
people's lives. We can't produce miracles
overnight. But we can bring a cup of
cool water to a thirsty soul, or a scoop of
laughter to a lonely heart.

Barbara Johnson

Values for Life

Someone very near you may need a helping hand or a kind word, so
keep your eyes open, and look for people who need your help, whether
at home, at church, or at school.

Timeless Wisdom for Godly Living

Do all the good you can. By all the means you can. In all the ways you can. In all the places you can. At all the times you can. To all the people you can. As long as ever you can.

John Wesley

Unless our belief in God causes us to help our fellowmen, our faith stands condemned.

Billy Graham

So let us try to do what makes peace and helps one another.
Romans 14:19 NCV

Make it a rule, and pray to God to help you to keep it, never, if possible, to lie down at night without being able to say: "I have made one human being at least a little wiser, or a little happier, or at least a little better this day."

Charles Kingsley

I never look at the masses as my responsibility. I look at the individual. I can love only one person at a time. I can feed only one person at a time. Just one, one, one. You get closer to Christ by coming closer to each other.

Mother Teresa

More Words from God's Word

Do not withhold good from those who deserve it when it's in your power to help them.

Proverbs 3:27 NLT

The one who blesses others is abundantly blessed; those who help others are helped.

Proverbs 11:25 MSG

Then a Samaritan traveling down the road came to where the hurt man was. When he saw the man, he felt very sorry for him. The Samaritan went to him, poured olive oil and wine on his wounds, and bandaged them. Then he put the hurt man on his own donkey and took him to an inn where he cared for him.

Luke 10:33-34 NCV

Carry one another's burdens; in this way you will fulfill the law of Christ.

Galatians 6:2 HCSB

My Values for Life

I believe God wants me to help others.

I understand that whenever I help other people, I feel better about myself.

I look for creative ways to lend a helping hand whenever I can.

Check Your Value		
High	Med.	Low
—	—	—
—	—	—
—	—	—

Helping Others

The Temple of God That Belongs to You

Didn't you realize that your body is a sacred place, the place of the Holy Spirit? Don't you see that you can't live however you please, squandering what God paid such a high price for? The physical part of you is not some piece of property belonging to the spiritual part of you.

1 Corinthians 6:19 MSG

What does worship have to do with fitness? That depends on how you define worship. If you consider worship to be a "Sunday-only" activity, an activity that occurs only inside the four walls of your local church, then fitness and worship may seem totally unrelated. But, if you view worship as an activity that impacts every facet of your life—if you consider worship to be something far more than a "one-day-a week" obligation—then you understand that every aspect of your life is a form of worship. And that includes keeping your body physically fit.

Make no mistake: All of mankind (including you) is engaged in worship . . . of one kind or another. The question is not whether we worship, but what we worship. Some of us choose to worship our Heavenly Father. The result is a plentiful harvest of joy, peace, and abundance. Others distance themselves from God by placing the desire for personal gratification above the need for spiritual gratification. To do so can be a terrible mistake with eternal consequences.

Every day provides opportunities to put God where He belongs: at the center of our lives. When we do so, we worship not just with our words, but also with our deeds. And one way that we can honor our Heavenly Father is by treating our bodies with care and respect.

The Bible makes it clear: "Your body is the temple of the Holy Spirit" (1 Corinthians 6:19 NLT). Treat it that way. And consider your fitness regimen to be one way—a very important way—of worshipping God.

Maximum physical health happens when the body—with all its chemicals, parts, and systems—is functioning as closely to the way God designed it to function.

Dr. Walt Larimore

Values for Life

Fitness tips in the Bible: God's Word is full of advice about health, moderation, and sensible living. When you come across these passages, take them to heart and put them to use.

Timeless Wisdom for Godly Living

Too much food and too little exercise leads to fat buildup, while less food and more exercise leads to a healthier, slimmer body.

Jim Maxwell

Our minds have been endowed with an incredible ability to affect the functioning and overall health of our bodies.

Dr. Kenneth Cooper

Whatever you eat or drink or whatever you do, you must do all for the glory of God.
1 Corinthians 10:31 NLT

If you desire to improve your physical well-being and your emotional outlook, increasing your faith can help you.

John Maxwell

Jesus Christ is the One by Whom, for Whom, through Whom everything was made. Therefore, He knows what's wrong in your life and how to fix it.

Anne Graham Lotz

God wants you to give Him your body. Some people do foolish things with their bodies. God wants your body as a holy sacrifice.

Warren Wiersbe

More Words from God's Word

I discipline my body like an athlete, training it to do what it should. Otherwise, I fear that after preaching to others I myself might be disqualified.

1 Corinthians 9:27 NLT

Therefore, brothers, by the mercies of God, I urge you to present your bodies as a living sacrifice, holy and pleasing to God; this is your spiritual worship.

Romans 12:1 HCSB

The Lord is the strength of my life.

Psalm 27:1 KJV

The Lord will take away from thee all sickness.

Deuteronomy 7:15 KJV

My Values for Life

	Check Your Value		
	High	Med.	Low
I believe that God wants me to treat my body with care.	—	—	—
I understand the importance of staying physically fit.	—	—	—
I believe God will help me become a more physically fit person if I will ask for His help.	—	—	—

The Rule That Is Golden

Do to others what you want them to do to you.

Matthew 7:12 NCV

The noted American theologian Phillips Brooks advised, "Be such a man, and live such a life, that if every man were such as you, and every life a life like yours, this earth would be God's Paradise." One tangible way to make the world a more godly place is to spread kindness wherever we go.

Sometimes, when we feel happy or generous, we find it easy to be kind. Other times, when we are discouraged or tired, we can scarcely summon the energy to utter a single kind word. But, God's commandment is clear: He intends that we make the conscious choice to treat others with kindness and respect, no matter our circumstances, no matter our emotions.

For believers, kindness is not an option; it is a commandment. In the Gospel of Matthew, Jesus declares, "In everything, therefore, treat people the same way you want them to treat you, for this is the Law and the Prophets" (Matthew 7:12 NASB). Jesus did not say, "In some things, treat people as you wish to be treated." And, He did not say, "From time to time, treat others with kindness." Christ said that we should treat others as we wish to be treated in everything.

This, of course, is a tall order indeed, but as Christians, we are commanded to do our best.

Today, as you consider all the things that Christ has done in your life, honor Him by being a little kinder than necessary. Honor Him by slowing down long enough to say an extra word of encouragement to someone who needs it. Honor Him by picking up the phone and calling a distant friend . . . for no reason other than to say, "I'm thinking of you." Honor Christ by following His commandment and obeying the Golden Rule. He expects no less, and He deserves no less.

It is one of the most beautiful compensations of life that no one can sincerely try to help another without helping herself.

Barbara Johnson

Values for Life

How would you feel? When you're trying to decide how to treat another person, ask yourself this question: "How would I feel if somebody treated me that way?" Then, treat the other person the way that you would want to be treated.

Timeless Wisdom for Godly Living

Anything done for another is done for oneself.

Pope John Paul II

Here lies the tremendous mystery—that God should be all-powerful, yet refuse to coerce. He summons us to cooperation. We are honored in being given the opportunity to participate in His good deeds. Remember how He asked for help in performing His miracles: Fill the water pots, stretch out your hand, distribute the loaves.

Elisabeth Elliot

Don't be selfish . . . . Be humble,
thinking of others as better than yourself.
Philippians 2:3 TLB

We ought not to be weary of doing little things for the love of God, who regards not the greatness of the work, but the love with which it is performed.

Brother Lawrence

Make the most of today. Translate your good intentions into actual good deeds.

Grenville Kleiser

More Words from God's Word

Each of you should look not only to your own interests, but also to the interest of others.

Philippians 2:4 NIV

Yes indeed, it is good when you truly obey our Lord's royal command found in the Scriptures: "Love your neighbor as yourself."

James 2:8 NLT

And let us not grow weary while doing good, for in due season we shall reap if we do not lose heart.

Galatians 6:9 NKJV

See that no one pays back evil for evil, but always try to do good to each other and to everyone else.

1 Thessalonians 5:15 TLB

My Values for Life

I believe that it is important to treat all people with respect and kindness.

When dealing with other people, I believe that it is important to try to "walk in their shoes."

I find that when I treat others with respect, I feel better about myself.

Check Your Value		
High	Med.	Low
—	—	—
—	—	—
—	—	—

The Power of Simplicity

A simple life in the Fear-of-God is better than a rich life with a ton of headaches.

Proverbs 15:16 MSG

Y ou live in a world where simplicity is in short supply. Think for a moment about the complexity of your life and compare it to the lives of your ancestors. Certainly, you are the beneficiary of many technological innovations, but these innovations have a price: in all likelihood, your world is highly complex. Consider the following:

1. From the moment you wake up in the morning until the time you lay your head on the pillow at night, you are the target of an endless stream of advertising information. Each message is intended to grab your attention in order to convince you to purchase things you didn't know you needed (and probably don't!).

2. Essential aspects of your life, including personal matters such as health care, are subject to an ever-increasing flood of rules and regulations.

3. Unless you take firm control of your time and your life, you may be overwhelmed by a tidal wave of complexity that threatens your happiness.

Is yours a life of moderation or accumulation? Are you more interested in the possessions you can acquire or in the person you can become? The answers to these questions will determine the direction of your day and, in time, the direction of your life. If your material possessions are somehow distancing you from God, discard them. If your outside interests leave you too little time for your family or your Creator, slow down the merry-go-round, or better yet, get off the merry-go-round completely. Remember: God wants your full attention, and He wants it today, so don't let anybody or anything get in His way.

The characteristic of the life of a saint is essentially elemental simplicity.

Oswald Chambers

Values for Life

Simplicity now: Perhaps you think that the more stuff you acquire, the happier you'll be. If so, think again. Too much stuff means too many headaches, so start simplifying now.

Timeless Wisdom for Godly Living

There is absolutely no evidence that complexity and materialism lead to happiness. On the contrary, there is plenty of evidence that simplicity and spirituality lead to joy, a blessedness that is better than happiness.

Dennis Swanberg

Prescription for a happier and healthier life: resolve to slow down your pace; learn to say no gracefully; resist the temptation to chase after more pleasure, more hobbies, and more social entanglements.

James Dobson

We brought nothing into the world, so we can take nothing out. But, if we have food and clothes, we will be satisfied with that.

1 Timothy 6:7-8 NCV

In the name of Jesus Christ who was never in a hurry, we pray, O God, that You will slow us down, for we know that we live too fast. With all eternity before us, make us take time to live—time to get acquainted with You, time to enjoy Your blessing, and time to know each other.

Peter Marshall

More Words from God's Word

No one can serve two masters. The person will hate one master and love the other, or will follow one master and refuse to follow the other. You cannot serve both God and worldly riches.

Matthew 6:24 NCV

The Lord preserves the simple; when I was brought low, he saved me.

Psalm 116:6 RSV

Then Jesus said to them, "Be careful and guard against all kinds of greed. Life is not measured by how much one owns."

Luke 12:15 NCV

The law of the LORD is perfect, converting the soul: the testimony of the LORD is sure, making wise the simple.

Psalm 19:7 KJV

My Values for Life

	Check Your Value	
High	Med.	Low

I value the benefits of simplicity.

The world leads me toward a life of complexity and stress. God leads me toward simplicity and peace.

I understand that the accumulation of material possessions does not ensure a joyful life; it is my relationship with God that brings me abundance and joy.

God's Surprising Plans

"I say this because I know what I am planning for you," says the Lord.
"I have good plans for you, not plans to hurt you.
I will give you hope and a good future."

Jeremiah 29:11 NCV

The Bible makes it clear: God's got a plan—a whopper of a plan—and you play a vitally important role in it. But here's the catch: God won't force His plans upon you; you've got to figure things out for yourself . . . or not.

As a Christian, you should ask yourself this question: "How closely can I make my plans match God's plans?" The more closely you manage to follow the path that God intends for your life, the better.

Do you have questions or concerns about the future? Take them to God in prayer. Do you have hopes and expectations? Talk to God about your dreams. Are you carefully planning for the days and weeks ahead? Consult God as you establish your priorities. Turn every concern over to your Heavenly Father, and sincerely seek His guidance—prayerfully, earnestly, and often. Then, listen for His answers . . . and trust the answers that He gives.

Sometimes, God's plans are crystal clear, but other times, He may lead you through the wilderness before He delivers you to the

Promised Land. So be patient, keep praying, and keep seeking His will for your life. When you do, you'll be amazed at the marvelous things that an all-powerful, all-knowing God can do.

You cannot out-dream God.

John Eldredge

Values for Life

Waiting faithfully for God's plan to unfold is more important than understanding God's plan. Ruth Bell Graham once said, "When I am dealing with an all-powerful, all-knowing God, I, as a mere mortal, must offer my petitions not only with persistence, but also with patience. Someday I'll know why." Even when you can't understand God's plans, you must trust Him and never lose faith!

Timeless Wisdom for Godly Living

Every man's life is a plan of God.

Horace Bushnell

What God has started in all of us He has promised to finish.

Gloria Gaither

I'm convinced that there is nothing that can happen to me in this life that is not precisely designed by a sovereign Lord to give me the opportunity to learn to know Him.

Elisabeth Elliot

> *A man's heart plans his way,*
> *but the Lord directs his steps.*
> *Proverbs 16:9 NKJV*

God has no problems, only plans. There is never panic in heaven.

Corrie ten Boom

Mark it down: things do not "just happen." There is a God-arranged plan for this world of ours, which includes a specific plan for you.

Charles Swindoll

More Words from God's Word

God is working in you to help you want to do and be able to do what pleases him.

Philippians 2:13 NCV

There is one thing I always do. Forgetting the past and straining toward what is ahead, I keep trying to reach the goal and get the prize for which God called me . . . .

Philippians 3:13-14 NCV

Those who listen to instruction will prosper; those who trust the LORD will be happy.

Proverbs 16:20 NLT

You will show me the way of life, granting me the joy of your presence and the pleasures of living with you forever.

Psalm 16:11 NLT

My Values for Life

Since God created me, I will trust Him to know what's best for me.

Since I believe God has a plan for my day, I set aside quiet time each morning in order to seek His will for my life.

Since I trust that God's plans have eternal ramifications, I will seek His will for my life.

Check Your Value		
High	Med.	Low
—	—	—
—	—	—
—	—	—

He Is Here

Again, this is God's command: to believe in his personally named Son,
Jesus Christ. He told us to love each other, in line with the original
command. As we keep his commands, we live deeply and surely in him,
and he lives in us. And this is how we experience his deep and
abiding presence in us: by the Spirit he gave us.

1 John 3:23-24 MSG

Do you ever wonder if God really hears your prayers? If so, you're in good company: lots of very faithful Christians have wondered the same thing. In fact, some of the biggest heroes in the Bible had their doubts—and so, perhaps, will you. But when you have your doubts, remember this: God isn't on vacation, and He hasn't moved out of town. God isn't taking a coffee break, and He isn't snoozing on the couch. He's right here, right now, listening to your thoughts and prayers, watching over your every move.

Do you schedule a regular meeting each day with your Creator? You should. During these moments of stillness, you will gain direction, perspective, and peace—God's peace.

The comforting words of Psalm 46:10 remind us to "Be still, and know that I am God." When we do so, we sense the loving presence of our Heavenly Father, and we are comforted by the certain knowledge that God is not far away . . . and He isn't even nearby. He is, quite literally, here. And it's up to each of us to sense His presence.

Sometimes, you will allow yourself to become very busy, and that's when you may be tempted to ignore God. But, when you quiet yourself long enough to acknowledge His presence, God will touch your heart and restore your spirits. By the way, He's ready to talk right now. Are you?

The tender eyes of God perpetually see us. He has never stopped noticing.

Angela Thomas

Values for Life

Having trouble hearing God? If so, slow yourself down, tune out the distractions, and listen carefully. God has important things to say; your task is to be still and listen.

Timeless Wisdom for Godly Living

The Lord Jesus by His Holy Spirit is with me, and the knowledge of His presence dispels the darkness and allays any fears.

Bill Bright

Through the death and broken body of Jesus Christ on the Cross, you and I have been given access to the presence of God when we approach Him by faith in prayer.

Anne Graham Lotz

The Lord is with you when you are with Him. If you seek Him, He will be found by you.
2 Chronicles 15:2 HCSB

You're busy with all the pressures of the world around you, but in that busyness you're missing the most important element of all— God's ongoing presence that is available to you.

Bill Hybels

What a comfort to know that God is present there in your life, available to meet every situation with you, that you are never left to face any problem alone.

Vonette Bright

More Words from God's Word

From one man He has made every nation of men to live all over the earth and has determined their appointed times and the boundaries of where they live, so that they might seek God, and perhaps they might reach out and find Him, though He is not far from each one of us.

Acts 17:26-27 HCSB

Let your character be free from the love of money, being content with what you have; for He Himself has said, "I will never desert you, nor will I ever forsake you."

Hebrews 13:5 NASB

Fear not, for I am with you; Be not dismayed, for I am your God. I will strengthen you.

Isaiah 41:10 NKJV

Draw close to God, and God will draw close to you.

James 4:8 NLT

My Values for Life

	Check Your Value	
High	Med.	Low

I place value upon quiet communication with God.
— — —

I believe it is important to have a regular time of prayer and reflection.
— — —

I am comforted by God's presence, and I seek Him often.
— — —

A Willingness to Serve

The greatest among you will be your servant.
Whoever exalts himself will be humbled,
and whoever humbles himself will be exalted.

Matthew 23:11-12 HCSB

We live in a world that glorifies power, prestige, fame, and money. But the words of Jesus teach us that the most esteemed men and women are not the widely acclaimed leaders of society; the most esteemed among us are the humble servants of society.

When we experience success, it's easy to puff out our chests and proclaim, "I did that!" But it's wrong. Whatever "it" is, God did it, and He deserves the credit. As Christians, we have been refashioned and saved by Jesus Christ, and that salvation came not because of our own good works but because of God's grace.

Dietrich Bonhoeffer was correct when he observed, "It is very easy to overestimate the importance of our own achievements in comparison with what we owe others." In other words, reality breeds humility.

Are you willing to become a humble servant for Christ? Are you willing to pitch in and make the world a better place, or are you determined to keep all your blessings to yourself? The answer to these questions will determine the quantity and the quality of the service you render to God—and to His children.

Today, you may feel the temptation to take more than you give. You may be tempted to withhold your generosity. Or you may be tempted to build yourself up in the eyes of your friends. Resist these temptations. Instead, serve your friends quietly and without fanfare. Find a need and fill it . . . humbly. Lend a helping hand . . . anonymously. Share a word of kindness . . . with quiet sincerity. As you go about your daily activities, remember that the Savior of all humanity made Himself a servant, and you, as His follower, must do no less.

If you aren't serving, you're just existing, because life is meant for ministry.

Rick Warren

Values for Life

Whatever your age, whatever your circumstances, you can serve: Each stage of life's journey is a glorious opportunity to place yourself in the service of the One who is the Giver of all blessings. As long as you live, you should honor God with your service to others.

Timeless Wisdom for Godly Living

God does not do anything with us, only through us.

Oswald Chambers

Christianity, in its purest form, is nothing more than seeing Jesus. Christian service, in its purest form, is nothing more than imitating him who we see. To see his Majesty and to imitate him: that is the sum of Christianity.

Max Lucado

If anyone serves Me, let him follow Me;
and where I am, there My servant will be also.
If anyone serves Me, him My Father will honor.
John 12:26 NKJV

Service is love in overalls!

Anonymous

Without God, we cannot. Without us, God will not.

St. Augustine

As Jesus repeatedly declared, the path to greatness in the kingdom follows the route he himself pioneered, self-sacrificial service to others. As a result, the prominent persons in God's new order will be those who are servants of all.

Stanley Grenz

More Words from God's Word

Think of yourselves the way Christ Jesus thought of himself. He had equal status with God but didn't think so much of himself that he had to cling to the advantages of that status no matter what. Not at all. When the time came, he set aside the privileges of deity and took on the status of a slave, became human! Having become human, he stayed human. It was an incredibly humbling process. He didn't claim special privileges. Instead he lived a selfless, obedient life and then died a selfless, obedient death, and the worst kind of death at that: a crucifixion.

Philippians 2:5-8 MSG

Therefore, since we receive a kingdom which cannot be shaken, let us show gratitude, by which we may offer to God an acceptable service with reverence and awe . . . .

Hebrews 12:28 NASB

So prepare your minds for service and have self-control.

1 Peter 1:13 NCV

My Values for Life

Christ was a humble servant, and I value the importance of following His example.

Greatness in God's kingdom relates to service, not status.

I am proactive in my search to find ways to help others.

	Check Your Value	
High	Med.	Low
—	—	—
—	—	—
—	—	—

Trusting God's Love

This is how much God loved the world: He gave his Son,
his one and only Son. And this is why: so that no one need be destroyed;
by believing in him anyone can have a whole and lasting life.

John 3:16 MSG

How much does God love you? As long as you're alive, you'll never be able to figure it out because God's love is just too big to comprehend. But this much we know: God loves you so much that He sent His Son Jesus to come to this earth and to die for you! And, when you accepted Jesus into your heart, God gave you a gift that is more precious than gold: the gift of eternal life.

Sometimes, in the crush of your daily activities, God may seem far away, but He is not. God is with you night and day; He knows your thoughts and your prayers. And, when you earnestly seek Him, you will find Him because He is here, waiting patiently for you to reach out to Him.

St. Augustine observed, "God loves each of us as if there were only one of us." Do you believe those words? Do you seek to have an intimate, one-on-one relationship with your Heavenly Father, or are you satisfied to keep Him at a "safe" distance?

God's love is bigger and more powerful than anybody can imagine, but His love is very real. So do yourself a favor right now:

accept God's love with open arms and welcome His Son Jesus into your heart. When you do, your life will be changed today, tomorrow, and forever.

Joy comes from knowing God loves me and knows who I am and where I'm going . . . that my future is secure as I rest in Him.

James Dobson

God is the sunshine that warms us, the rain that melts the frost and waters the young plants. The presence of God is a climate of strong and bracing love, always there.

Joan Arnold

Values for Life

Remember: God's love for you is too big to understand with your brain . . . but it's not too big to feel with your heart.

Timeless Wisdom for Godly Living

We can all humbly say in the sincerity of faith, "I am loved; I am called; I am secure."

Franklin Graham

Because we are rooted and grounded in love, we can be relaxed and at ease, knowing that our acceptance is not based on our performance or our perfect behavior.

Joyce Meyer

We love Him because He first loved us.
1 John 4:19 NKJV

If God had a refrigerator, your picture would be on it. If he had a wallet, your photo would be in it. He sends you flowers every spring and a sunrise every morning.

Max Lucado

A joyful heart is like the sunshine of God's love, the hope of eternal happiness, a burning flame of God . . . . And if we pray, we will become that sunshine of God's love—in our own home, the place where we live, and in the world at large.

Mother Teresa

More Words from God's Word

For he chose us in him before the creation of the world to be holy and blameless in his sight. In love he predestined us to be adopted as his sons through Jesus Christ, in accordance with his pleasure and will . . . .

Ephesians 1:4-5 NIV

Now return to the LORD your God, For He is gracious and compassionate, slow to anger, abounding in lovingkindness.

Joel 2:13 NASB

This is what real love is: It is not our love for God; it is God's love for us in sending his Son to be the way to take away our sins.

1 John 4:10 NCV

We know how much God loves us, and we have put our trust in him. God is love, and all who live in love live in God, and God lives in them.

1 John 4:16 NLT

My Values for Life

I believe that God loves me.

I understand the importance of a loving relationship with God by spending time with Him.

I understand the importance of sharing God's love with my family and friends.

Check Your Value		
High	Med.	Low

God's Love

God's Gift of Grace

For by grace you are saved through faith, and this is not from yourselves; it is God's gift—not from works, so that no one can boast.

Ephesians 2:8-9 HCSB

God's grace is not earned . . . thank goodness! To earn God's love and His gift of eternal life would be far beyond the abilities of even the most righteous man or woman. Thankfully, grace is not an earthly reward for righteous behavior; it is a blessed spiritual gift which can be accepted by believers who dedicate themselves to God through Christ. When we accept Christ into our hearts, we are saved by His grace.

The familiar words of Ephesians 2:8 make God's promise perfectly clear: It is by grace we have been saved, through faith. We are saved not because of our good deeds but because of our faith in Christ.

God's grace is the ultimate gift, and we owe to Him the ultimate in thanksgiving. Let us praise the Creator for His priceless gift, and let us share the Good News with all who cross our paths. We return our Father's love by accepting His grace and by sharing His message and His love.

Have you thanked God today for blessings that are too numerous to count? Have you offered Him your heartfelt prayers and your wholehearted praise? If not, it's time to slow down and offer a prayer of thanksgiving to the One who has given you life on earth and life eternal.

If you are a thoughtful Christian, you will be a thankful Christian. No matter your circumstances, you owe God so much more than you can ever repay, and you owe Him your heartfelt thanks. So thank Him . . . and keep thanking Him, today, tomorrow and forever.

> The life of faith is a daily exploration of the constant and countless ways in which God's grace and love are experienced.
>
> *Eugene Peterson*

Values for Life

God's Grace Is Always Available: Jim Cymbala writes, "No one is beyond His grace. No situation, anywhere on earth, is too hard for God." If you sincerely seek God's grace, He will give it freely. So ask, and you will receive.

Timeless Wisdom for Godly Living

Though the details may differ from story to story, we are all sinners—saved only by the wonderful grace of God.

Gloria Gaither

Living by grace inspires a growing consciousness that I am what I am in the sight of Jesus and nothing more. It is His approval that counts.

Brennan Manning

> *For the law was given through Moses;*
> *grace and truth came through Jesus Christ.*
> John 1:17 HCSB

Costly grace is the treasure hidden in the field; for the sake of it, a man will gladly go and sell all that he has. It is costly because it costs a man his life, and it is grace because it gives a man the only true life.

Dietrich Bonhoeffer

I want first of all . . . to be at peace with myself. I want a singleness of eye, a purity of intention, a central core to my life . . . . I want, in fact—to borrow from the language of the saints—to live "in grace" as much of the time as possible.

Anne Morrow Lindbergh

More Words from God's Word

For the grace of God has been revealed, bringing salvation to all people. And we are instructed to turn from godless living and sinful pleasures. We should live in this evil world with self-control, right conduct, and devotion to God, while we look forward to that wonderful event when the glory of our great God and Savior, Jesus Christ, will be revealed.

Titus 2:11-12 NLT

For all have sinned and fall short of the glory of God, and are justified freely by his grace through the redemption that came by Christ Jesus.

Romans 3:23-24 NIV

But He gives more grace. Therefore He says: "God resists the proud, But gives grace to the humble."

James 4:6 NKJV

So let us come boldly to the throne of our gracious God. There we will receive his mercy, and we will find grace to help us when we need it.

Hebrews 4:16 NLT

My Values for Life

I believe that God has graced me with many gifts.

I believe in the importance of sharing the transforming message of God's gift of grace.

I believe that His grace is sufficient for my needs.

Check Your Value		
High	Med.	Low
___	___	___
___	___	___
___	___	___

On Beyond Failure

For though a righteous man falls seven times, he rises again . . . .

Proverbs 24:16 NIV

From time to time, all of us face life-altering disappointments that leave us breathless. Oftentimes, these disappointments come unexpectedly, leaving us with more questions than answers. But even when we don't have all the answers, God does. Whatever our circumstances, whether we stand atop the highest mountain or wander through the darkest valley, God is ready to protect us, to comfort us, and to heal us. Our task is to let Him.

Life is a tapestry of events: some grand, some not-so-grand, some disappointing, and some tragic. During the happy times, we are tempted to take our blessings for granted (a temptation that we must resist with all our might). But, during life's difficult days, we discover precisely what we're made of. And more importantly, we discover what our faith is made of.

If your faith is being tested by difficult circumstances, here are some things to consider:

Your Response: God wants you to respond to life's disappointing moments with an attitude of obedience. No matter how difficult your circumstances, God calls you to obey the instructions that are contained in His Holy Word. He wants you to remain hopeful (Psalm 31:24); He instructs you to remain faithful to Him, and He wants you to be courageous (Matthew 8:26). God also expects you to forgive those who have injured you (Matthew 6:14-15), and He wants you to treat others with kindness and gentleness (Ephesians 4:32). These commandments are often difficult to obey—especially when you feel angry or hurt—but obey them you must . . . otherwise you invite God's disapproval.

Your Lessons: What does God want you to learn from your disappointments? Plenty! Every disappointing chapter of life has important lessons to teach, but no one can learn those lessons for you—you must learn them for yourself. And with God's help, you will.

Your Future: If you've endured a life-altering disappointment, you may have good reason to ask, "Where do you want me to go from here, Lord?" And you may rest assured that, in time, your Heavenly Father will answer you. His answer may not come immediately, and it may not come in a way that you expect, but of this you can be certain: if you sincerely ask, God will answer (Matthew 7:7-8).

When tough times arrive, you should learn from your experiences, and you should prayerfully seek God's guidance for the future. Then, you should tackle the work at hand—the difficult and rewarding work of overcoming your disappointments. When you do your part, you can be certain that God will do His part. And you can be sure that in time, your loving Heavenly Father will turn your stumbling blocks into stepping stones.

Every achievement worth remembering is
stained with the blood of diligence
and scarred by the wounds of disappointment.

Charles Swindoll

The difference between winning and losing is
how we choose to react to disappointment.

Barbara Johnson

If your hopes are being disappointed just now,
it means that they are being purified.

Oswald Chambers

No matter how badly we have failed,
we can always get up and begin again.
Our God is the God of new beginnings.

Warren Wiersbe

Values for Life

Failure Isn't Permanent . . . Unless You Fail to Bounce Back. So pick yourself up, dust yourself off, and trust God. He will make it right. Warren Wiersbe had this advice: "No matter how badly we have failed, we can always get up and begin again. Our God is the God of new beginnings." And don't forget: the best time to begin again is now.

Timeless Wisdom for Godly Living

Why should I ever resist any delay or disappointment, any affliction or oppression or humiliation, when I know God will use it in my life to make me like Jesus and to prepare me for heaven?

Kay Arthur

The next time you're disappointed, don't panic and don't give up. Just be patient and let God remind you he's still in control.

Max Lucado

> *But as for you, be strong and do not give up,*
> *for your work will be rewarded.*
> 2 Chronicles 15:7 NIV

The amazing thing is that God follows us into the blackened ruins of our failed dreams, our misbegotten mirages, into the house of cards that has collapsed on us in some way and he speaks, not with the chastisement we feel we deserve, but of all things, with tenderness.

Paula Rinehart

Recently I've been learning that life comes down to this: God is in everything. Regardless of what difficulties I am experiencing at the moment, or what things aren't as I would like them to be, I look at the circumstances and say, "Lord, what are you trying to teach me?"

Catherine Marshall

More Words from God's Word

Let us not become weary in doing good, for at the proper time we will reap a harvest if we do not give up.

Galatians 6:9 NIV

You need to persevere so that when you have done the will of God, you will receive what he has promised.

Hebrews 10:36 NIV

Be of good courage, and he shall strengthen your heart, all ye that hope in the LORD.

Psalm 31:24 KJV

Unto thee, O my strength, will I sing: for God is my defense, and the God of my mercy.

Psalm 59:17 KJV

My Values for Life

I value the need to keep my disappointments in perspective.

I believe that adversity can be a stepping stone to success.

I believe that I have much to learn from adversity.

Check Your Value		
High	Med.	Low
—	—	—
—	—	—
—	—	—

The Cheerful Giver

Freely you have received, freely give.

Matthew 10:8 NKJV

Your blessings from God are too numerous to count. Those blessings include life, family, friends, talents, and possessions, for starters. But, your greatest blessing—a gift that is yours for the asking—is God's gift of salvation through Christ Jesus. Today, give thanks for your blessings and show your thanks by using them and by sharing them.

The thread of generosity is woven—completely and inextricably—into the very fabric of Christ's teachings. He reminded His followers that, "Whatever you did for one of the least of these brothers of mine, you did for me" (Matthew 25:40 NIV). The implication is clear: If we genuinely seek to follow Christ, we must share our time, our possessions, our love, and our faith.

Today, as you go about the business of living your life, be more generous than necessary. This world needs every bit of kindness and generosity that springs from the hearts of believers like you. Your generosity will glorify the One who has been so generous to you, and your kindness will touch the hearts of friends and strangers alike. And, be assured that no good deed is ever wasted. Every time that you share a kind word or a generous gift with another human being, you have also shared it with the Savior of the world.

In gratitude for God's gift of life to us
we should share that gift with others.
The art of giving encompasses many areas.
It is an outgoing, overflowing way of life.

Wilferd Peterson

A cheerful giver does not count the cost of
what he gives. His heart is set on pleasing and
cheering him to whom the gift is given.

Juliana of Norwich

Values for Life

There is a direct relationship between generosity and joy—the more
you give to others, the more joy you will experience for yourself.

Timeless Wisdom for Godly Living

Do things for others and you'll find your self-consciousness evaporating like morning dew on a Missouri cornfield in July.

Dale Carnegie

But the proper aim of giving is to put the recipient in a state where he no longer needs our gift.

C. S. Lewis

You can't out give God. If folks who claim to be Christian would all start tithing income, there would never be another cake walk, Bingo game, rummage sale, or spaghetti supper because folks who love God would dip down into their pockets and give back a portion of what he's blessed them with, and they'd cut out all this stuff.

Jerry Clower

God loves a cheerful giver.
2 Corinthians 9:7 NIV

It is when we give ourselves to be a blessing that we can specially count on the blessing of God. It is when we draw near to God as the friend of the poor and the perishing that we may count on His friendliness.

Andrew Murray

More Words from God's Word

In every way I've shown you that by laboring like this, it is necessary to help the weak and to keep in mind the words of the Lord Jesus, for He said, "It is more blessed to give than to receive."

Acts 20:35 HCSB

Be generous: Invest in acts of charity. Charity yields high returns.

Ecclesiastes 11:1 MSG

Give away your life; you'll find life given back, but not merely given back —given back with bonus and blessing. Giving, not getting, is the way. Generosity begets generosity.

Luke 6:38 MSG

Never walk away from someone who deserves help; your hand is God's hand for that person.

Proverbs 3:27 MSG

My Values for Life

	Check Your Value		
	High	Med.	Low

I understand the importance of being a cheerful giver.

— — —

I understand the need to give generously with my time.

— — —

I understand the importance of being a faithful steward of my talents.

— — —

Forgiving and Forgetting

In prayer there is a connection between what God does and what you do. You can't get forgiveness from God, for instance, without also forgiving others. If you refuse to do your part, you cut yourself off from God's part.

Matthew 6:14-15 MSG

Do you value the role that forgiveness can play in your life? Hopefully so. But even if you're a dedicated believer, you may have a difficult time forgiving those who have hurt you. If you're one of those folks who, despite your best intentions, has a difficult time forgiving and forgetting, you are not alone.

Life would be much simpler if we humans could forgive people "once and for all" and be done with it. But forgiveness is seldom that easy. For most people, the decision to forgive is straightforward, but the process of forgiving is more difficult. Forgiveness is a journey that requires effort, time, perseverance, and prayer.

Sometimes, it's not "the other person" whom you need to forgive; it's yourself. If you've made mistakes (and who among us hasn't?), perhaps you're continuing to bear a grudge against the person in the mirror. If so, here's a three-step process for resolving those feelings:

(1) Stop the harmful behavior that is the source of your self-directed anger. (2) Seek forgiveness from God (and from any people

whom you may have hurt). (3) Ask God to cleanse your heart of all bitterness and regret . . . and keep asking Him until your feelings of anger and regret are gone.

If there exists even one person, alive or dead, whom you have not forgiven (and that includes yourself), follow God's commandment: forgive that person today. And remember that bitterness, anger, and regret are not part of God's plan for your life. Forgiveness is.

Perhaps you need a refresher course in the art of forgiveness. If so, it's time to open your Bible and your heart. When you do, you'll discover that God can heal your broken spirit. Don't expect forgiveness to be easy or quick, but rest assured that with God as your partner, you can forgive . . . and you will.

At the heart of God is the desire
to give and to forgive.

Richard Foster

Values for Life

Holding a grudge? Drop it. Never expect other people to be more forgiving than you are. And remember: the best time to forgive is now.

Timeless Wisdom for Godly Living

Miracles broke the physical laws of the universe; forgiveness broke the moral rules.

Philip Yancey

If you can't seem to forgive someone, pray for that person and keep praying for him or her until, with God's help, you've removed the poison of bitterness from your heart.

Marie T. Freeman

Whoever forgives someone's sin makes a friend, but gossiping about the sin breaks up friendships.
Proverbs 17:9 NCV

There is nothing, absolutely nothing, that God will not forgive. You cannot "out-sin" His forgiveness. You cannot "out-sin" the love of God.

Kathy Troccoli

What keeps us from forgiving each other? We are prone to focus on the problem or the wrong done to us rather than on the person who wronged us.

Franklin Graham

More Words from God's Word

Smart people know how to hold their tongue; their grandeur is to forgive and forget.

Proverbs 19:11 MSG

Then Peter came to him and asked, "Lord, how often should I forgive someone who sins against me? Seven times?" "No!" Jesus replied, "seventy times seven!

Matthew 18:21-22 NLT

But when you are praying, first forgive anyone you are holding a grudge against, so that your Father in heaven will forgive your sins, too.

Mark 11:25 NLT

Don't pick on people, jump on their failures, criticize their faults—unless, of course, you want the same treatment. Don't condemn those who are down; that hardness can boomerang. Be easy on people; you'll find life a lot easier.

Luke 6:37 MSG

My Values for Life

I understand that when I ask God for forgiveness, He grants it.

Because God has forgiven me, I can forgive myself.

Because God has forgiven me, I can forgive others.

Check Your Value		
High	Med.	Low
—	—	—
—	—	—
—	—	—

Following Christ

As Jesus went on from there, he saw a man named Matthew sitting at the tax collector's booth. "Follow me," he told him, and Matthew got up and followed him.

Matthew 9:9 NIV

Whom are you going to walk with today? Are you going to walk with people who worship the ways of the world? Or are you going to walk with the Son of God? Jesus walks with you. Are you walking with Him? Hopefully, you will choose to walk with Him today and every day of your life.

Jesus loved you so much that He endured unspeakable humiliation and suffering for you. How will you respond to Christ's sacrifice? Will you take up His cross and follow Him (Luke 9:23), or will you choose another path? When you place your hopes squarely at the foot of the cross, and when you place Jesus squarely at the center of your life, you will be blessed.

The 19th-century writer Hannah Whitall Smith observed, "The crucial question for each of us is this: What do you think of Jesus, and do you yet have a personal acquaintance with Him?" Indeed, the answer to that question determines the quality, the course, and the direction of our lives today and for all eternity.

Today provides another glorious opportunity to place yourself in the service of the One from Galilee. May you seek His will, may you trust His word, and may you walk in His footsteps—now and forever—amen.

Think of this—we may live together with Him here and now, a daily walking with Him who loved us and gave Himself for us.

Elisabeth Elliot

Imagine the spiritual strength the disciples drew from walking hundreds of miles with Jesus . . . 3 John 4.

Jim Maxwell

Values for Life

If you want to be a little more like Christ . . . learn about His teachings, follow in His footsteps, and obey His commandments.

Timeless Wisdom for Godly Living

It takes real faith to begin to live the life of heaven while still upon the earth, for this requires that we rise above the law of moral gravitation and bring to our everyday living the high wisdom of God. And since this wisdom is contrary to that of the world, conflict is bound to result. This, however; is a small price to pay for the inestimable privilege of following Christ.

A. W. Tozer

Then said Jesus unto his disciples,
If any man will come after me, let him deny himself,
and take up his cross, and follow me.
Matthew 16:24 KJV

Christ is like a river that is continually flowing. There are always fresh supplies of water coming from the fountain-head, so that a man may live by it and be supplied with water all his life. So Christ is an ever-flowing fountain; he is continually supplying his people, and the fountain is not spent. They who live upon Christ may have fresh supplies from him for all eternity; they may have an increase of blessedness that is new, and new still, and which never will come to an end.

Jonathan Edwards

More Words from God's Word

*Are you tired? Worn out? Burned out on religion? Come to me. Get
away with me and you'll recover your life. I'll show you how to take a
real rest. Walk with me and work with me . . . watch how I do it. Learn
the unforced rhythms of grace. I won't lay anything heavy or ill-fitting on
you. Keep company with me and you'll learn to live freely and lightly.*

Matthew 11:28-30 MSG

*No one can serve two masters. Either he will hate the one and love the
other, or he will be devoted to the one and despise the other.*

Matthew 6:24 NIV

*Follow Me, He told them, "and I will make you fishers of men!"
Immediately they left their nets and followed Him.*

Matthew 4:19-20 HCSB

My Values for Life

I believe that my relationship with Jesus should be one of
servant and Master. I am the servant and He's the Master.

I believe that it is important for me to attempt to follow
in Christ's footsteps, despite my imperfections.

I believe there is a joyful abundance that is mine when
I follow Christ.

Check Your Value		
High	Med.	Low
—	—	—
—	—	—
—	—	—

A Lifetime of Learning

*Whoever listens to what is taught will succeed,
and whoever trusts the Lord will be happy.*

Proverbs 16:20 NCV

Whether you're 19 or 119, you've still got lots to learn. Even if you're very wise, God isn't finished with you yet, and He isn't finished teaching you important lessons about life here on earth and life eternal.

God does not intend for you to be a stagnant believer. Far from it! God wants you to continue growing as a person and as a Christian every day that you live. And make no mistake: both spiritual and intellectual growth are possible during every stage of life.

Are you a curious Christian who has committed yourself to the regimen of regular Bible study, or do you consult your Bible on a hit-or-miss basis? The answer to this question will be an indication of the extent to which you allow God to direct the course of your life.

As a spiritual being, you have the potential to grow in your personal knowledge of the Lord every day that you live. You can do so through prayer, through worship, through an openness to God's Holy Spirit, and through a careful study of God's Holy Word. Your Bible contains powerful prescriptions for everyday living. If you sincerely seek to walk with God, you should commit yourself to the thoughtful study of His teachings.

Do you seek to live a life of righteousness and wisdom? If so, you must continue to study the ultimate source of wisdom: the Word of God. You must associate, day in and day out, with godly men and women. And, you must act in accordance with your beliefs. When you study God's Word and live according to His commandments, you will become wise . . . and you will serve as a shining example to your friends, to your family, and to the world.

The wonderful thing about God's schoolroom is that we get to grade our own papers. You see, He doesn't test us so He can learn how well we're doing. He tests us so we can discover how well we're doing.

Charles Swindoll

Values for Life

Never Stop Learning. Think of it like this: when you're through learning, you're through.

Timeless Wisdom for Godly Living

Today is yesterday's pupil.

Thomas Fuller

The wise man gives proper appreciation in his life to this past. He learns to sift the sawdust of heritage in order to find the nuggets that make the current moment have any meaning.

Grady Nutt

*A wise man will hear and increase in learning,
and a man of understanding will acquire wise counsel.*
Proverbs 1:5 NASB

The doorstep to the temple of wisdom is a knowledge of our own ignorance.

C. H. Spurgeon

Knowledge is power.

Francis Bacon

It's the things you learn after you know it all that really count.

Vance Havner

More Words from God's Word

For this very reason, make every effort to supplement your faith with goodness, goodness with knowledge, knowledge with self-control, self-control with endurance, endurance with godliness.

2 Peter 1:5-6 HCSB

The fear of the Lord is the beginning of knowledge, but fools despise wisdom and discipline.

Proverbs 1:7 NIV

Apply your heart to discipline And your ears to words of knowledge.

Proverbs 23:12 NASB

By wisdom a house is built, and through understanding it is established; through knowledge its rooms are filled with rare and beautiful treasures.

Proverbs 24:3-4 NIV

My Values for Life

	Check Your Value	
High	Med.	Low

I value the importance of learning.

God's wisdom sometimes opposes the world's wisdom; I choose God's wisdom.

I can learn from the past, but I don't choose to live in the past.

Strength from Family

*Let the Word of Christ—the Message—have the run of the house.
Give it plenty of room in your lives. Instruct and direct one another using
good common sense. And sing, sing your hearts out to God! Let every
detail in your lives—words, actions, whatever—be done in the name of
the Master, Jesus, thanking God the Father every step of the way.*

Colossians 3:16-17 MSG

Do you sometimes take your family for granted? If so, welcome to the club. At times, it's surprisingly easy to ignore the people we love the most. After all, we know that they'll still love us no matter what we do. But whenever we ignore our loved ones, we're doing a big disservice to our loved ones and to ourselves.

A loving family is a treasure from God. If God has blessed you with a close-knit, supportive clan, offer a word of thanks to your Creator because He has given you one of His most precious earthly possessions. Your obligation, in response to God's gift, is to treat your family in ways that are consistent with His commandments.

You live in a fast-paced, demanding world, a place where life can be difficult and pressures can be intense. As those pressures build, you may tend to focus so intently upon your obligations that you lose sight, albeit temporarily, of your spiritual and emotional needs (that's one reason why a regular daily devotional time is so important; it offers a badly-needed dose of perspective).

So the next time your family life becomes a little stressful, remember this: That little band of men, women, kids, and babies is a priceless treasure on temporary loan from the Father above. And it's your responsibility to praise God for that gift—and to act accordingly.

It matters that we should be true to one another, be loyal to what is a family— only a little family in the great Household, but still a family, with family love alive in it and action as a living bond.

Amy Carmichael

Values for Life

Since you love them, tell them so! Let your family members know that you love them by the things you say and the things you do. And, never take your family for granted; they deserve your very best treatment!

Timeless Wisdom for Godly Living

Money can build or buy a house. Add love to that, and you have a home. Add God to that, and you have a temple. You have "a little colony of the kingdom of heaven."

Anne Ortlund

I like to think of my family as a big, beautiful patchwork quilt—each of us so different yet stitched together by love and life experiences.

Barbara Johnson

Love must be without hypocrisy. Detest evil;
cling to what is good. Show family affection to
one another with brotherly love.
Outdo one another in showing honor.
Romans 12:9-10 HCSB

Never give your family the leftovers and crumbs of your time.

Charles Swindoll

The only true source of meaning in life is found in love for God and his son Jesus Christ, and love for mankind, beginning with our own families.

James Dobson

More Words from God's Word

You must choose for yourselves today whom you will serve . . . as for me and my family, we will serve the Lord.

Joshua 24:15 NCV

Their first responsibility is to show godliness at home and repay their parents by taking care of them. This is something that pleases God very much.

1 Timothy 5:4 NLT

Love never gives up. Love cares more for others than for self. Love doesn't want what it doesn't have. Love doesn't strut, Doesn't have a swelled head, Doesn't force itself on others, Isn't always "me first," Doesn't fly off the handle, Doesn't keep score of the sins of others, Doesn't revel when others grovel, Takes pleasure in the flowering of truth, Puts up with anything, Trusts God always, Always looks for the best, Never looks back, But keeps going to the end.

1 Corinthians 13:4-7 MSG

My Values for Life

	Check Your Value	
High	Med.	Low

I place a high priority on spending time with my family.

| — | — | — |

I think that my family should make God its number one priority.

| — | — | — |

I look for ways to say, and to show, my family I love them.

| — | — | — |

A Foundation of Faith

I can do everything through him that gives me strength.

Philippians 4:13 NIV

When we trust God, we should trust Him without reservation. But sometimes, especially during life's darker days, trusting God may be difficult. Yet this much is certain: whatever our circumstances, we must continue to plant the seeds of faith in our hearts, trusting that in time God will bring forth a bountiful harvest. Planting the seeds for that harvest requires work, which is perfectly okay with God. After all, He never gives us burdens that we cannot bear.

It is important to remember that the work required to build and sustain our faith is an ongoing process. Corrie ten Boom advised, "Be filled with the Holy Spirit; join a church where the members believe the Bible and know the Lord; seek the fellowship of other Christians; learn and be nourished by God's Word and His many promises. Conversion is not the end of your journey—it is only the beginning."

The work of nourishing your faith can and should be joyful work. The hours that you invest in Bible study, prayer, meditation, and worship should be times of enrichment and celebration. And, as you continue to build your life upon a foundation of faith, you will discover that the journey toward spiritual maturity lasts a lifetime. As a child of God, you are never fully "grown": instead, you can continue "growing up" every day of your life. And that's exactly what God wants you to do.

God doesn't always change the circumstances, but He can change us to meet the circumstances. That's what it means to live by faith.

Warren Wiersbe

Values for Life

Faith is more than a feeling: Faith sometimes results in good feelings, but Kay Arthur correctly writes, "We are to live by faith, not feelings."

Timeless Wisdom for Godly Living

What pleases God is faith, and the weakest faith is better than no faith. Faith does not look at itself. Looking unto Jesus, we find that He meets our needs and proves that we have faith.

Vance Havner

I am truly grateful that faith enables me to move past the question of "Why?"

Zig Ziglar

> *The righteous will live by his faith.*
> Habakkuk 2:4 NIV

Just as our faith strengthens our prayer life, so do our prayers deepen our faith. Let us pray often, starting today, for a deeper, more powerful faith.

Shirley Dobson

I want my life to be a faith-filled leap into his arms, knowing he will be there—not that everything will go as I want, but that he will be there and that this will be enough.

Sheila Walsh

Faith means believing in advance what will only make sense in reverse.

Philip Yancey

More Words from God's Word

The fundamental fact of existence is that this trust in God, this faith, is the firm foundation under everything that makes life worth living.

Hebrews 11:1 MSG

It is impossible to please God apart from faith. And why? Because anyone who wants to approach God must believe both that he exists and that he cares enough to respond to those who seek him.

Hebrews 11:6 MSG

Let us run with endurance the race that is set before us, fixing our eyes on Jesus, the author and perfecter of faith.

Hebrews 12:1-2 NASB

Jesus said, "Because you have seen Me, you have believed. Blessed are those who believe without seeing."

John 20:29 HCSB

My Values for Life

I will build my faith each day through regular Bible study and prayer.

I will praise God many times each day for His blessings.

I am determined to seek God's will and to follow God's Son.

	Check Your Value	
High	Med.	Low
—	—	—
—	—	—
—	—	—

faith

Possibilities According to God

For with God nothing will be impossible.

Luke 1:37 NKJV

We live in a world of infinite possibilities. But sometimes, because of limited faith and limited understanding, we wrongly assume that God cannot or will not intervene in the affairs of mankind. Such assumptions are simply wrong.

Are you afraid to ask God to do big things in your life? Is your faith threadbare and worn? If so, it's time to abandon your doubts and reclaim your faith—faith in yourself, faith in your abilities, faith in your future, and faith in your Heavenly Father.

Catherine Marshall notes that, "God specializes in things thought impossible." And make no mistake: God can help you do things you never dreamed possible . . . your job is to let Him.

Sometimes, when we read of God's miraculous works in Biblical times, we tell ourselves, "That was then, but this is now." When we do so, we are mistaken. God is with His children "now" just as He was "then." He is right here, right now, performing miracles. And, He will continue to work miracles in our lives to the extent we are willing to trust in Him and to the extent those miracles fit into the fabric of His divine plan.

Miracles—both great and small—happen around us all day every day, but usually, we're too busy to notice. Some miracles, like the twinkling of a star or the glory of a sunset, we take for granted. Other miracles, like the healing of a terminally sick patient, we chalk up to fate or to luck. We assume, quite incorrectly, that God is "out there" and we are "right here." Nothing could be farther from the truth.

Do you lack the faith that God can work miracles in your own life? If so, it's time to reconsider. Instead of doubting God, trust His power, and expect His miracles. Then, wait patiently . . . because something miraculous is about to happen.

He who trusts in himself is lost.
He who trusts in God can do all things.

Alphonsus Liguori

Values for Life

If you're looking for miracles . . . you'll find them. If you're not, you won't.

Timeless Wisdom for Godly Living

You were born with tremendous potential. When you were born again through faith in Jesus Christ, God added spiritual gifts to your natural talents.

Warren Wiersbe

When you believe that nothing significant can happen through you, you have said more about your belief in God than you have said about yourself.

Henry Blackaby

No eye has seen, no ear has heard, no mind has conceived what God has prepared for those who love him.
1 Corinthians 2:9 NIV

Everyone has inside himself a piece of good news! The good news is that you really don't know how great you can be, now much you can live, what you can accomplish, and what your potential is.

Anne Frank

When you say a situation or a person is hopeless, you are slamming the door in the face of God.

Charles L. Allen

More Words from God's Word

Is anything too hard for the Lord?

Genesis 18:14 NKJV

If you have faith as a mustard seed, you will say to this mountain, "Move from here to there," and it will move; and nothing will be impossible for you.

Matthew 17:20 NKJV

I am able to do all things through Him who strengthens me.

Philippians 4:13 HCSB

If God be for us, who can be against us?

Romans 8:31 KJV

The things which are impossible with men are possible with God.

Luke 18:27 KJV

My Values for Life

	Check Your Value	
High	Med.	Low

I expect God to work miracles.

— — —

When I place my faith in God, life becomes a grand adventure.

— — —

Worship reminds me of the awesome power of God. I worship Him daily and seek to allow Him to work through me.

— — —

The Power of Encouragement

But encourage each other daily, while it is still called today,
so that none of you is hardened by sin's deception.

Hebrews 3:13 HCSB

ife is a team sport, and all of us need occasional pats on the back from our teammates. This world can be a difficult place, a place where many of our friends and family members are troubled by the challenges of everyday life. And since we cannot always be certain who needs our help, we should strive to speak helpful words to all who cross our paths.

In his letter to the Ephesians, Paul writes, "Do not let any unwholesome talk come out of your mouths, but only what is helpful for building others up according to their needs, that it may benefit those who listen" (vv. 29 NIV). This passage reminds us that, as Christians, we are instructed to choose our words carefully so as to build others up through wholesome, honest encouragement. How can we build others up? By celebrating their victories and their accomplishments. As the old saying goes, "When someone does something good, applaud—you'll make two people happy."

Genuine encouragement should never be confused with pity. God intends for His children to lead lives of abundance, joy, celebration and praise—not lives of self-pity or regret. So we must guard ourselves against hosting (or joining) the "pity parties" that so often accompany difficult times. Instead, we must encourage each other to have faith—first in God and His only begotten Son—and then in our own abilities to use the talents God has given us for the furtherance of His kingdom and for the betterment of our own lives.

As a faithful follower of Jesus, you have every reason to be hopeful, and you have every reason to share your hopes with others. When you do, you will discover that hope, like other human emotions, is contagious. So do the world (and yourself) a favor: Look for the good in others and celebrate the good that you find. When you do, you'll be a powerful force of encouragement to your friends and family . . . and a worthy servant to your God.

We urgently need people who encourage
and inspire us to move toward God
and away from the world's enticing pleasures.

Jim Cymbala

Values for Life

Sometimes, even a very few words can make a very big difference. As Fanny Crosby observed, "A single word, if spoken in a friendly spirit, may be sufficient to turn one from dangerous error."

Timeless Wisdom for Godly Living

Encouraging others means helping people, looking for the best in them, and trying to bring out their positive qualities.

John Maxwell

Words. Do you fully understand their power? Can any of us really grasp the mighty force behind the things we say? Do we stop and think before we speak, considering the potency of the words we utter?

Joni Eareckson Tada

> *Kind words are like honey—*
> *sweet to the soul and healthy for the body.*
> Proverbs 16:24 NLT

God is still in the process of dispensing gifts, and He uses ordinary individuals like us to develop those gifts in other people.

Howard Hendricks

No journey is complete that does not lead through some dark valleys. We can properly comfort others only with the comfort we ourselves have been given by God.

Vance Havner

More Words from God's Word

Let's see how inventive we can be in encouraging love and helping out, not avoiding worshipping together as some do but spurring each other on.

Hebrews 10:24-25 MSG

Watch the way you talk. Let nothing foul or dirty come out of your mouth. Say only what helps, each word a gift.

Ephesians 4:29 MSG

So don't lose a minute in building on what you've been given, complementing your basic faith with good character, spiritual understanding, alert discipline, passionate patience, reverent wonder, warm friendliness, and generous love, each dimension fitting into and developing the others.

2 Peter 1:5-7 MSG

My Values for Life

I believe that God wants me to encourage other people.

I carefully think about the words I speak so that every word might be a "gift of encouragement" to others.

I understand that my words reflect my heart. I will guard my heart so that my words will be pleasing to God.

Check Your Value		
High	Med.	Low
—	—	—
—	—	—
—	—	—

During Those Difficult Days

We take the good days from God—why not also the bad days?

Job 2:10 MSG

A ll of us face those occasional days when the traffic jams and the dog gobbles the homework. But, when we find ourselves overtaken by the minor frustrations of life, we must catch ourselves, take a deep breath, and lift our thoughts upward. Although we are here on earth struggling to rise above the distractions of the day, we need never struggle alone. God is here— eternally and faithfully, with infinite patience and love—and, if we reach out to Him, He will restore perspective and peace to our souls.

Sometimes even the most devout Christians can become discouraged, and you are no exception. After all, you live in a world where expectations can be high and demands can be even higher.

If you find yourself enduring difficult circumstances, remember that God remains in His heaven. If you become discouraged with the direction of your day or your life, lift your thoughts and prayers to Him. He is a God of possibility, not negativity. He will guide you through your difficulties and beyond them. Then, you can thank the Giver of all things good for blessings that are simply too numerous to count.

When life is difficult,
God wants us to have a faith that
trusts and waits.

Kay Arthur

Looking back, I can see that
the most exciting events of my life
have all risen out of trouble.

Catherine Marshall

Values for Life

If It Wasn't for Trouble . . . we might think we could handle our
lives by ourselves. Jim Cymbala writes, "Trouble is one of God's great
servants because it reminds us how much we continually need the
Lord." We should thank the Lord for challenges that bring us closer to
Him.

Timeless Wisdom for Godly Living

The truth is that even in the midst of trouble, happy moments swim by us every day, like shining fish waiting to be caught.

Barbara Johnson

Measure the size of the obstacles against the size of God.

Beth Moore

> *Be joyful because you have hope.*
> *Be patient when trouble comes, and pray at all times.*
> *Romans 12:12 NCV*

We sometimes fear to bring our troubles to God because we think they must seem small to Him. But, if they are large enough to vex and endanger our welfare, they are large enough to touch His heart of love.

R. A. Torrey

Often the trials we mourn are really gateways into the good things we long for.

Hannah Whitall Smith

More Words from God's Word

Then they cried out to the LORD in their trouble; He saved them out of their distresses.

Psalm 107:19 NASB

I have told you these things, so that in me you may have peace. In this world you will have trouble. But take heart! I have overcome the world.

John 16:33 NIV

Dear brothers and sisters, whenever trouble comes your way, let it be an opportunity for joy. For when your faith is tested, your endurance has a chance to grow. So let it grow, for when your endurance is fully developed, you will be strong in character and ready for anything.

James 1:2-4 NLT

My Values for Life

When I encounter difficulties, I understand the importance of looking for solutions.

I tackle problems sooner rather than later.

When I encounter difficulties, I work to solve the problems instead of worrying about them.

Check Your Value		
High	Med.	Low
—	—	—
—	—	—
—	—	—

Above and Beyond Anger

Foolish people lose their tempers, but wise people control theirs.

Proverbs 29:11 NCV

I f you're like most people, you know a thing or two about anger. After all, everybody gets mad occasionally, and you're no exception.

Anger is a natural human emotion that is sometimes necessary and appropriate. Even Jesus became angry when confronted with the moneychangers in the temple: "And Jesus entered the temple and drove out all those who were buying and selling in the temple, and overturned the tables of the moneychangers and the seats of those who were selling doves" (Matthew 21:12 NASB).

Righteous indignation is an appropriate response to evil, but God does not intend that anger should rule our lives. Far from it. God intends that we turn away from anger whenever possible and forgive our neighbors just as we seek forgiveness for ourselves.

Life is full of frustrations: some great and some small. On occasion, you, like Jesus, will confront evil, and when you do, you may respond as He did: vigorously and without reservation. But, more often your frustrations will be of the more mundane variety. As long as you live here on earth, you will face countless opportunities to lose your temper over small, relatively insignificant events: a traffic jam, an inconsiderate comment, or a broken promise. When you are tempted to lose your temper over the minor inconveniences of life, don't. Instead of turning up the heat, walk away. Turn away from anger, hatred, bitterness, and regret. Turn, instead, to God. When you do, you'll be following His commandments and giving yourself a priceless gift . . . the gift of peace.

Anger is the noise of the soul;
the unseen irritant of the heart;
the relentless invader of silence.

Max Lucado

Values for Life

Time Out!: If you become angry, the time to step away from the situation is before you say unkind words or do unkind things—not after. It's perfectly okay to place yourself in "time out" until you can calm down.

Timeless Wisdom for Godly Living

Acrid bitterness inevitably seeps into the lives of people who harbor grudges and suppress anger, and bitterness is always a poison.

Lee Strobel

Anger is a kind of temporary madness.

St. Basil the Great

Take no action in a furious passion. It's putting to sea in a storm.

Thomas Fuller

When you are angry, do not sin, and be sure to stop being angry before the end of the day. Do not give the devil a way to defeat you.
Ephesians 4:26-27 NCV

The only justifiable anger defends the great, glorious, and holy nature of our God.

John MacArthur

Why lose your temper if, by doing so, you offend God, annoy other people, give yourself a bad time . . . and, in the end, have to find it again?

Josemaria Escriva

More Words from God's Word

Now you must rid yourselves of all such things as these: anger, rage, malice . . . .

Colossians 3:8 NIV

Therefore I want the men in every place to pray, lifting up holy hands, without wrath and dissension.

1 Timothy 2:8 NASB

My dear brothers and sisters, always be willing to listen and slow to speak. Do not become angry easily, because anger will not help you live the right kind of life God wants.

James 1:19-20 NCV

Then Jesus went into the temple of God and drove out all those who bought and sold in the temple, and overturned the tables of the money changers and the seats of those who sold doves.

Matthew 21:12 NKJV

My Values for Life

I understand the importance of controlling my temper.

I understand the need to accept my past and forgive those who have hurt me.

When I forgive others, I feel better about myself.

Check Your Value		
High	Med.	Low
—	—	—
—	—	—
—	—	—

The Dating Game

Regarding life together and getting along with each other,
you don't need me to tell you what to do.
You're God-taught in these matters. Just love one another!

1 Thessalonians 4:9 MSG

Is God a part of your dating life? Hopefully so. If you sincerely want to know God, then you should date people who feel the same way.

If you're still searching for Mr. or Mrs. Right (while trying to avoid falling in love with Mr. or Mrs. Wrong), be patient, be prudent, and be picky. Look for someone whose values you respect, whose behavior you approve of, and whose faith you admire. Remember that appearances can be deceiving and tempting, so watch your step. And when it comes to the important task of building a lifetime relationship with the guy or girl of your dreams, pray about it!

If you happen to be one of those very lucky ones who have already fallen madly in love with the same wonderful person who has (praise the Lord!) already fallen madly in love with you, say a great big thanks to the Matchmaker in heaven. But if you haven't yet found a soul mate who honors both you and God, don't fret. Just keep trusting your Father in heaven, and keep yourself open to the direction in which He is leading you. And remember: When it comes to your dating life, God wants to give His approval—or not—but He won't give it until He's asked. So ask, listen, and decide accordingly.

There may be no trumpet sound or loud applause when we make a right decision, just a calm sense of resolution and peace.

Gloria Gaither

It is possible to be close to people physically and miles away from them spiritually.

Warren Wiersbe

Values for Life

Be choosy: Don't "settle" for second-class treatment—you deserve someone who values you as a person . . . and shows it. (Psalm 40:1)

Timeless Wisdom for Godly Living

I don't buy the cliché that quality time is the most important thing. If you don't have enough quantity, you won't get quality.

Leighton Ford

We discover our role in life through our relationships with others.

Rick Warren

Do not be unequally yoked together with unbelievers. For what fellowship has righteousness with lawlessness? And what communion has light with darkness?

2 Corinthians 6:14 NKJV

Morality and immorality are not defined by man's changing attitudes and social customs. They are determined by the God of the universe, whose timeless standards cannot be ignored with impunity.

James Dobson

If God has you in the palm of his hand and your real life is secure in him, then you can venture forth— into the places and relationships, the challenges, the very heart of the storm—and you will be safe there.

Paula Rinehart

More Words from God's Word

And regardless of what else you put on, wear love. It's your basic, all-purpose garment. Never be without it. Let the peace of Christ keep you in tune with each other, in step with each other. None of this going off and doing your own thing. And cultivate thankfulness.

Colossians 3:14-15 MSG

A friend loves you all the time, and a brother helps in time of trouble.

Proverbs 17:17 NCV

As iron sharpens iron, a friend sharpens a friend.

Proverbs 27:17 NLT

This is my command: Love one another the way I loved you. This is the very best way to love. Put your life on the line for your friends.

John 15:12-13 MSG

My Values for Life

In my dating life, I desire to glorify God, so I pray for His guidance and follow it.

In my dating life, I go places where I am likely to bump into the kind of people I want to meet.

I don't feel compelled to date "just for the sake of dating." I believe that it's better to be dating nobody than to be dating the wrong person.

Check Your Value		
High	Med.	Low
—	—	—
—	—	—
—	—	—

Dating

Living Courageously

Be strong and brave, and do the work. Don't be afraid or discouraged,
because the Lord God, my God, is with you.
He will not fail you or leave you.

1 Chronicles 28:20 NCV

A storm rose quickly on the Sea of Galilee, and the disciples were afraid. Although they had seen Jesus perform many miracles, and although they had walked side by side with the Son of God, the disciples feared for their lives. So they turned to their Savior, and He calmed the waters and the wind.

Sometimes, we, like the disciples, feel threatened by the inevitable storms of life. When we are fearful, we, too, can turn to Christ for courage and for comfort. When we do so, He calms our fears just as surely as He calmed the winds and the waters two thousand years ago.

Billy Graham observed, "Down through the centuries, in times of trouble and trial, God has brought courage to the hearts of those who love Him. The Bible is filled with assurances of God's help and comfort in every kind of trouble which might cause fears to arise in the human heart. You can look ahead with promise, hope, and joy."

The next time you find your courage tested by the inevitable challenges of everyday living, remember that God is as near as your next breath. He is your shield and your strength; He is your protector and your deliverer. Call upon Him in your hour of need and then be comforted. Whatever your challenge, whatever your trouble, God can handle it. And will.

Perhaps I am stronger than I think.

Thomas Merton

Values for Life

Is your courage being tested? Cling tightly to God's promises, and pray. God can give you the strength to meet any challenge, and that's exactly what you should ask Him to do.

Timeless Wisdom for Godly Living

God did away with all my fear. It was time for someone to stand up—or in my case, sit down. So I refused to move.

Rosa Parks

God knows that the strength that comes from wrestling with our fear will give us wings to fly.

Paula Rinehart

Courage faces fear and thereby masters it. Cowardice represses fear and is thereby mastered by it.

Martin Luther King, Jr.

> *Therefore, being always of good courage . . .*
> *we walk by faith, not by sight.*
> *2 Corinthians 5:6-7 NASB*

What is courage? It is the ability to be strong in trust, in conviction, in obedience. To be courageous is to step out in faith—to trust and obey, no matter what.

Kay Arthur

Dreaming the dream of God is not for cowards.

Joey Johnson

More Words from God's Word

For God has not given us a spirit of fear, but of power and of love and of a sound mind.

2 Timothy 1:7 NKJV

The LORD himself goes before you and will be with you; he will never leave you nor forsake you. Do not be afraid; do not be discouraged.

Deuteronomy 31:8 NIV

Do not be afraid . . . I am your shield, your very great reward.

Genesis 15:1 NIV

Since God assured us, "I'll never let you down, never walk off and leave you," we can boldly quote, God is there, ready to help; I'm fearless no matter what. Who or what can get to me?

Hebrews 13:5-6 MSG

My Values for Life

	Check Your Value	
High	Med.	Low

I understand the importance of living courageously.

I overcome fear by praying, and then by facing my fears head on.

If I find myself in a situation that I cannot control, I turn my concerns over to God and leave the results up to Him.

Valuing Your Gifts

Each one has his own gift from God,
one in this manner and another in that.

1 Corinthians 7:7 NKJV

God knew precisely what He was doing when He gave you a unique set of talents and opportunities. And now, God wants you to use those talents for the glory of His kingdom. So here's the big question: will you choose to use those talents, or not?

Your Heavenly Father wants you to be a faithful steward of the gifts He has given you. But you live in a society that may encourage you to do otherwise. You face countless temptations to squander your time, your resources, and your talents. So you must be keenly aware of the inevitable distractions that can waste your time, your energy, and your opportunities.

Every day of your life, you have a choice to make: to nurture your talents or neglect them. When you choose wisely, God rewards your efforts, and He expands your opportunities to serve Him.

God has blessed you with unique opportunities to serve Him, and He has given you every tool that you need to do so. Today, accept this challenge: value the talent that God has given you, nourish it, make it grow, and share it with the world. After all, the best way to say "Thank You" for God's gifts is to use them.

In the great orchestra we call life,
you have an instrument and a song,
and you owe it to God to
play them both sublimely.

Max Lucado

Values for Life

Polishing your skills requires effort: Converting raw talent into polished skill usually requires work, and lots of it. God's Word clearly instructs you to do the hard work of refining your talents for the glory of His kingdom and the service of His people. So, we are wise to remember the old adage: "What you are is God's gift to you; what you become is your gift to God." And it's up to you to make sure that your gift is worthy of the Giver.

Timeless Wisdom for Godly Living

Discipline is the refining fire by which talent becomes ability.

Roy L. Smith

You are the only person on earth who can use your ability.

Zig Ziglar

God has given gifts to each of you from his great variety of spiritual gifts. Manage them well so that God's generosity can flow through you.

1 Peter 4:10 NLT

One thing taught large in the Holy Scriptures is that while God gives His gifts freely, He will require a strict accounting of them at the end of the road. Each man is personally responsible for his store, be it large or small, and will be required to explain his use of it before the judgment seat of Christ.

A. W. Tozer

God often reveals His direction for our lives through the way He made us . . . with a certain personality and unique skills.

Bill Hybels

Employ whatever God has entrusted you with, in doing good, all possible good, in every possible kind and degree.

John Wesley

More Words from God's Word

Do not neglect the spiritual gift that is within you . . . .

1 Timothy 4:14 NASB

Every good gift and every perfect gift is from above, and cometh down from the Father of lights.

James 1:17 KJV

The man who had received the five talents brought the other five. "Master," he said, "you entrusted me with five talents. See, I have gained five more." His master replied, "Well done, good and faithful servant! You have been faithful with a few things; I will put you in charge of many things. Come and share your master's happiness."

Matthew 25:20-21 NIV

My Values for Life

I believe that God wants me to take risks to do the work that He intends for me to do.

I believe that it is important to associate with people who encourage me to use my talents.

I believe that it is important to honor God by using the talents He has given me.

Check Your Value		
High	Med.	Low
—	—	—
—	—	—
—	—	—

Claiming Contentment in a Discontented World

I've learned by now to be quite content whatever my circumstances.
I'm just as happy with little as with much, with much as with little.
I've found the recipe for being happy whether full or
hungry, hands full or hands empty.

Philippians 4:11-12 MSG

Where can you find contentment? Is it a result of wealth, or power or beauty or fame? Hardly. Genuine contentment springs from a peaceful spirit, a clear conscience, and a loving heart (like yours!).

Our modern world seems preoccupied with the search for happiness. We are bombarded with messages telling us that happiness depends upon the acquisition of material possessions. These messages are false. Enduring peace is not the result of our acquisitions; it is the inevitable result of our dispositions. If we don't find contentment within ourselves, we will never find it outside ourselves.

Thus the search for contentment is an internal quest, an exploration of the heart, mind, and soul. You can find contentment—indeed you will find it—if you simply look in the right places. And the best time to start looking in those places is now.

Are you a contented Christian? If so, then you are well aware of the healing power of the risen Christ. But if your spirit is temporarily troubled, perhaps you need to focus less upon your own priorities and more upon God's priorities. When you do, you'll rediscover this life-changing truth: Genuine contentment begins with God . . . and ends there.

He is rich that is satisfied.

Thomas Fuller

Values for Life

Be contented where you are . . . even if it's not exactly where you want to end up. God has something wonderful in store for you—and remember that God's timing is perfect—so be patient, trust God, do your best, and expect the best.

Timeless Wisdom for Godly Living

We will never be happy until we make God the source of our fulfillment and the answer to our longings.

Stormie Omartian

If I could just hang in there, being faithful to my own tasks, God would make me joyful and content. The responsibility is mine, but the power is His.

Peg Rankin

Keep your lives free from the love of money and be content with what you have, because God has said, "Never will I leave you; never will I forsake you."
Hebrews 13:5 NIV

Contentment is difficult because nothing on earth can satisfy our deepest longing. We long to see God.

Max Lucado

Father and Mother lived on the edge of poverty, and yet their contentment was not dependent upon their surroundings. Their relationship to each other and to the Lord gave them strength and happiness.

Corrie ten Boom

More Words from God's Word

But godliness with contentment is a great gain. For we brought nothing into the world, and we can take nothing out. But if we have food and clothing, we will be content with these. But those who want to be rich fall into temptation, a trap, and many foolish and harmful desires, which plunge people into ruin and destruction.

1 Timothy 6:6-9 HCSB

A heart at peace gives life to the body, but envy rots the bones.

Proverbs 14:30 NIV

Satisfy us in the morning with your unfailing love, that we may sing for joy and be glad all our days.

Psalm 90:14 NIV

My Values for Life

	Check Your Value	
High	Med.	Low

I believe that peace with God is the starting point for a contented life.

I understand that contentment comes, not from my circumstances, but from my attitude.

I understand that one way to find contentment is to praise God continually and thank Him for His blessings.

Trusting the Quiet Voice

*Now the goal of our instruction is love from a pure heart,
a good conscience, and a sincere faith.*

1 Timothy 1:5 HCSB

It has been said that character is what we are when nobody is watching. How true. When we do things that we know aren't right, we try to hide them from our families and friends. But even then, God is watching.

Few things in life torment us more than a guilty conscience. And, few things in life provide more contentment than the knowledge that we are obeying God's commandments. A clear conscience is one of the rewards we earn when we obey God's Word and follow His will. When we follow God's will and accept His gift of salvation, our earthly rewards are never-ceasing, and our heavenly rewards are everlasting.

Billy Graham correctly observed, "Most of us follow our conscience as we follow a wheelbarrow. We push it in front of us in the direction we want to go." If that describes you, then here's a word of warning: both you and your wheelbarrow are headed for trouble.

Do you place a high value on the need to keep your conscience clear? If so, keep up the good work. But if you're tempted to do something that you'd rather the world not know about, remember this: You can sometimes keep secrets from other people, but you can never keep secrets from God. God knows what you think and what you do. And if you want to please Him, you must start with good intentions, a pure heart, and a clear conscience.

If you sincerely wish to honor your Father in heaven, follow His commandments. When you do, your character will take care of itself . . . and so will your conscience. Then, as you journey through life, you won't need to look over your shoulder to see who—besides God—is watching.

> God desires that we become spiritually healthy enough through faith to have a conscience that rightly interprets the work of the Holy Spirit.
>
> *Beth Moore*

Values for Life

The more important the decision . . . the more carefully you should listen to your conscience.

Timeless Wisdom for Godly Living

Every secret act of character, conviction, and courage has been observed in living color by our omniscient God.

Bill Hybels

God has revealed Himself in man's conscience. Conscience has been described as the light of the soul.

Billy Graham

Your conscience is your alarm system. It's your protection.

Charles Stanley

I always do my best to have a clear conscience toward God and men.
Acts 24:16 HCSB

A quiet conscience sleeps in thunder.

Thomas Fuller

There is a balance to be maintained in situations. That balance is the Holy Spirit within us to guide us into the truth of each situation and circumstance in which we find ourselves. He will provide us the wisdom to know when we are to be adaptable and adjustable and when we are to take a firm stand and be immovable.

Joyce Meyer

More Words from God's Word

Since, then, you have been raised with Christ, set your hearts on things above, where Christ is seated at the right hand of God. Set your minds on things above, not on earthly things.

Colossians 3:1-2 NIV

Let us come near to God with a sincere heart and a sure faith, because we have been made free from a guilty conscience, and our bodies have been washed with pure water.

Hebrews 10:22 NCV

Do not conform any longer to the pattern of this world, but be transformed by the renewing of your mind. Then you will be able to test and approve what God's will is—his good, pleasing and perfect will.

Romans 12:2 NIV

My Values for Life

I understand the value of a clear conscience.

I believe that it is important that I attune my thoughts to God's will for my life.

When I prepare to make an important decision, I listen to my conscience very carefully.

Check Your Value		
High	Med.	Low
—	—	—
—	—	—
—	—	—

The Power of Patience

Knowing God leads to self-control. Self-control leads to patient endurance, and patient endurance leads to godliness.

2 Peter 1:6 NLT

The dictionary defines the word "patience" as "the ability to be calm, tolerant, and understanding." If that describes you, you can skip the rest of this page. But, if you're like most of us, you'd better keep reading.

For most of us, patience is a hard thing to master. Why? Because we have lots of things we want, and we know precisely when we want them: NOW (if not sooner). But our Father in heaven has other ideas; the Bible teaches that we must learn to wait patiently for the things that God has in store for us, even when waiting is difficult.

We live in an imperfect world inhabited by imperfect people. Sometimes, we inherit troubles from others, and sometimes we create troubles for ourselves. On other occasions, we see other people "moving ahead" in the world, and we want to move ahead with them. So we become impatient with ourselves, with our circumstances, and even with our Creator.

Psalm 37:7 commands us to "rest in the Lord, and wait patiently for Him" (NKJV). But, for most of us, waiting patiently for Him is hard.

We are fallible human beings who seek solutions to our problems today, not tomorrow. Still, God instructs us to wait patiently for His plans to unfold, and that's exactly what we should do.

Sometimes, patience is the price we pay for being responsible adults, and that's as it should be. After all, think how patient our Heavenly Father has been with us. So the next time you find yourself drumming your fingers as you wait for a quick resolution to the challenges of everyday living, take a deep breath and ask God for patience. Be still before your Heavenly Father and trust His timetable: it's the peaceful way to live.

Waiting means going about our assigned tasks, confident that God will provide the meaning and the conclusions.

Eugene Peterson

Values for Life

The best things in life seldom happen overnight . . . Henry Blackaby writes, "The grass that is here today and gone tomorrow does not require much time to mature. A big oak tree that lasts for generations requires much more time to grow and mature. God is concerned about your life through eternity. Allow Him to take all the time He needs to shape you for His purposes. Larger assignments will require longer periods of preparation." How true!

Timeless Wisdom for Godly Living

No matter what we are going through, no matter how long the waiting for answers, of one thing we may be sure. God is faithful. He keeps His promises. What he starts, He finishes . . . including His perfect work in us.

Gloria Gaither

But if we look forward to something we don't have yet, we must wait patiently and confidently.

Romans 8:25 NLT

Be patient. When you feel lonely, stay with your loneliness. Avoid the temptation to let your fearful self run off. Let it teach you its wisdom; let it tell you that you can live instead of just surviving. Gradually you will become one, and you will find that Jesus is living in your heart and offering you all you need.

Henri Nouwen

Let God use times of waiting to mold and shape your character. Let God use those times to purify your life and make you into a clean vessel for His service.

Henry Blackaby and Claude King

More Words from God's Word

Patience and encouragement come from God. And I pray that God will help you all agree with each other the way Christ Jesus wants.

Romans 15:5 NCV

I wait quietly before God, for my salvation comes from him. He alone is my rock and my salvation, my fortress where I will never be shaken.

Psalm 62:1-2 NLT

Patience is better than strength.

Proverbs 16:32 NCV

For when the way is rough, your patience has a chance to grow. So let it grow, and don't try to squirm out of your problems.

James 1:3-4 TLB

My Values for Life

I take seriously the Bible's instructions to be patient.

I believe that patience is not idle waiting but that it is an activity that means being watchful as I wait for God to lead me.

Even when I don't understand the circumstances that confront me, I strive to wait patiently while serving the Lord.

Check Your Value		
High	Med.	Low
—	—	—
—	—	—
—	—	—

Comforting Those in Need

Blessed be the God and Father of our Lord Jesus Christ,
the Father of mercies and the God of all comfort.
He comforts us in all our affliction, so that we may be able
to comfort those who are in any kind of affliction,
through the comfort we ourselves receive from God.

2 Corinthians 1:3-4 HCSB

We live in a world that is, on occasion, a frightening place. Sometimes, we sustain life-altering losses that are so profound and so tragic that it seems we could never recover. But, with God's help and with the help of encouraging family members and friends, we can recover.

In times of need, God's Word is clear: as believers, we must offer comfort to those in need by sharing not only our courage but also our faith. As the renowned revivalist Vance Havner observed, "No journey is complete that does not lead through some dark valleys. We can properly comfort others only with the comfort wherewith we ourselves have been comforted of God."

In times of adversity, we are wise to remember the words of Jesus, who, when He walked on the waters, reassured His disciples, saying, "Take courage! It is I. Don't be afraid" (Matthew 14:27 NIV). Then, with Christ on His throne—and with trusted friends and loving family members at our sides—we can face our fears with courage and with faith.

So often we think that to be encouragers we have to produce great words of wisdom when, in fact, a few simple syllables of sympathy and an arm around the shoulder can often provide much needed comfort.

Florence Littauer

Values for Life

Silence is Okay: When you're offering comfort to a friend, your presence may be more important than your words. Sometimes, just being there is enough. If you're not sure what to say, don't.

Timeless Wisdom for Godly Living

When we honestly ask ourselves which person in our lives means the most to us, we often find that it is he who, instead of giving much advice, solutions, and cures, has chosen rather to share our pain and touch our wounds with a gentle and tender hand. The friend who can be silent with us in a moment of despair or confusion, who can stay with us in an hour of grief and bereavement, who can tolerate not knowing, not curing, not healing, and face us with the reality of our powerlessness, that is a friend who cares.

Henri Nouwen

Humble yourselves therefore under the mighty hand of God, so that He may exalt you in due time, casting all your care upon Him, because He cares about you.
1 Peter 5:6-7 HCSB

God's promises are medicine for the broken heart. Let Him comfort you. And, after He has comforted you, try to share that comfort with somebody else. It will do both of you good.

Warren Wiersbe

Discouraged people don't need critics. They hurt enough already. They don't need more guilt or piled-on distress. They need encouragement. They need a refuge, a willing, caring, available someone.

Charles Swindoll

More Words from God's Word

God, who comforts the downcast, comforted us . . . .

2 Corinthians 7:6 NIV

I will not leave you comfortless: I will come to you.

John 14:18 KJV

This is my comfort in my affliction: Your promise has given me life.

Psalm 119:50 HCSB

Even though I walk through the valley of the shadow of death, I will fear no evil, for you are with me; your rod and your staff, they comfort me.

Psalm 23:4 NIV

When I am filled with cares, Your comfort brings me joy.

Psalm 94:19 HCSB

My Values for Life

I understand the importance of offering comfort to my family and friends.

I believe that comforting others requires empathy and compassion.

I believe that comforting others requires my presence and patience.

Check Your Value		
High	Med.	Low
—	—	—
—	—	—
—	—	—

Becoming a Great Communicator

A wise man's heart guides his mouth, and his lips promote instruction.

Proverbs 16:23 NIV

Your skills as a communicator will have a profound impact upon your relationships, your career, and your life. The more quickly you learn how to communicate effectively, the more quickly you'll give yourself an instant jumpstart.

Would you like to become a better communicator? Here are seven simple rules that can help:

(1) Think First, Speak Second: If you blurt out the first thing that comes into your head, you may say things that are better left unsaid. (2) Learn to Be a Good Listener: If you want to be listened to, then you, too, must be a careful listener. (3) Use Words That Are Appropriate, Understandable, and Precise: Vague, imprecise speeches may be useful in international diplomacy, but not helpful in everyday communications between human beings. Remember the advice of Winston Churchill: "Short words are best and old words, when short, are best of all." (4) Don't Be a Complainer: You simply can't whine your way to the top, so don't even try. (5) Use All the Tools at Your Disposal and Be Flexible: sometimes face-to-face beats e-mail and vice versa. Sometimes, telephone beats face-to face; sometimes, the mail works best (especially for thank you notes). Use

all of the above to get your messages across. (6) Don't Say Things "Behind Someone's Back" That You Wouldn't Say Directly to that Person's Face: Gossip isn't nice, and it isn't smart since the people you talk about will eventually find out what you said, and they won't forget. (7) Be a Trustworthy Communicator: Don't hedge the truth, don't omit important facts, and don't make promises that you can't keep. If you shade the truth, people always find out anyway, and they remember.

Today, make this promise to yourself: vow to be an honest, effective, encouraging communicator at work, at home, and everyplace in between. Speak wisely, not impulsively. Use words of kindness and praise, not words of anger or derision. Learn how to be truthful without being cruel. Remember that you have the power to heal others or to injure them, to lift others up or to hold them back. And when you learn how to lift them up, you'll soon discover that you've lifted yourself up, too.

We should ask ourselves three things before we speak: Is it true? Is it kind? Does it glorify God?

Billy Graham

Values for Life

Be Brief: longwinded monologues, although satisfying to the speaker, are usually torture for the audience.

Timeless Wisdom for Godly Living

Part of good communication is listening with the eyes as well as with the ears.

Josh McDowell

Attitude and the spirit in which we communicate are as important as the words we say.

Charles Stanley

> *A gentle answer turns away wrath,*
> *but a harsh word stirs up anger.*
> *Proverbs 15:1 NIV*

The first duty of love is to listen.

Paul Tillich

Expressed affection is the best of all methods to use when you want to light a glow in someone's heart and to feel it in your own.

Ruth Statford Peale

Does your message end with one point like a sword, or does it end like a broom with a thousand straws?

Vance Havner

More Words from God's Word

Let your speech be alway with grace . . . .

Colossians 4:6 KJV

Set a guard, O LORD, over my mouth; Keep watch over the door of my lips.

Psalm 141:3 NASB

A word aptly spoken is like apples of gold in settings of silver.

Proverbs 25:11 NIV

Kind words are like honey—sweet to the soul and healthy for the body.

Proverbs 16:24 NLT

The tongue that brings healing is a tree of life, but a deceitful tongue crushes the spirit.

Proverbs 15:4 NIV

My Values for Life

I understand the importance of being a good communicator.

I understand the need to be a good listener.

I understand the need for honesty and candor.

Check Your Value		
High	Med.	Low
—	—	—
—	—	—
—	—	—

The Joys of Friendship

As iron sharpens iron, a friend sharpens a friend.

Proverbs 27:17 NLT

The dictionary defines the word "friend" as "a person who is attached to another by feelings of affection or personal regard." This definition is accurate, as far as it goes, but when we examine the deeper meaning of friendship, many more descriptors come to mind: trustworthiness, loyalty, helpfulness, kindness, understanding, forgiveness, encouragement, humor, and cheerfulness, to mention but a few. Needless to say, our trusted friends and family members can help us discover God's unfolding purposes for our lives. Our task is to enlist our friends' wisdom, their cooperation, their honesty, and their encouragement.

An old familiar hymn begins, "What a friend we have in Jesus." No truer words were ever penned. Jesus is the sovereign friend and ultimate savior of mankind. Just as Christ has been—and will always be—the ultimate friend to His flock, so should we be Christ-like in our love and devotion to our own little flock of friends and neighbors. When we share the love of Christ, we share a priceless gift. As loyal friends, we must do no less.

As you consider the many blessings that God has given you, remember to thank Him for the friends He has chosen to place along your path. Seek their guidance, and, when asked, never withhold yours. Then, as you travel through life with trusted companions by your side, you will bless them, and they will richly bless you.

Loyal Christian friendship is ordained by God. Throughout the Bible, we are reminded to love one another, to care for one another, and to treat one another as we wish to be treated. So remember the important role that Christian friendship plays in God's plans for His kingdom and for your life. Resolve to be a trustworthy, loyal friend. And, treasure the people in your life who are loyal friends to you. Friendship is, after all, a glorious gift, praised by God. Give thanks for that gift and nurture it.

Friendship between the friends of Jesus of Nazareth is unlike any other friendship.

Stephen Neill

Values for Life

Remember the first rule of friendship: it's the Golden one, and it starts like this: "Do unto others . . . ." (Matthew 7:12)

Timeless Wisdom for Godly Living

The bond of human friendship has a sweetness of its own, binding many souls together as one.

St. Augustine

Friendship fills a deep well within me with fresh water. When I celebrate my friendships, it's like dropping a huge rock into the well. It splashes that water everywhere, on everyone else in my life.

Nicole Johnson

Greater love has no one than this,
that he lay down his life for his friends.
John 15:13 NIV

Perhaps the greatest treasure on earth and one of the only things that will survive this life is human relationships: old friends. We are indeed rich if we have friends. Friends who have loved us through the problems and heartaches of life. Deep, true, joyful friendships. Life is too short and eternity too long to live without old friends.

Gloria Gaither

The glory of friendship is not the outstretched hand, or the kindly smile, or the joy of companionship. It is the spiritual inspiration that comes to one when he discovers that someone else believes in him and is willing to trust him with his friendship.

Corrie ten Boom

More Words from God's Word

A friend loves you all the time, and a brother helps in time of trouble.

Proverbs 17:17 NCV

Beloved, if God so loved us, we also ought to love one another.

1 John 4:11 NKJV

*So don't lose a minute in building on what you've been given,
complementing your basic faith with good character, spiritual
understanding, alert discipline, passionate patience, reverent wonder,
warm friendliness, and generous love, each dimension fitting into and
developing the others.*

2 Peter 1:5-7 MSG

A man's counsel is sweet to his friend.

Proverbs 27:9 NASB

My Values for Life

	Check Your Value	
High	Med.	Low

I understand the importance of building close friendships.

In building friendships, I emphasize the need for mutual
honesty and mutual trust.

Because I want to cultivate my friendships, I make the
effort to spend time with my friends.

Cheerful Christianity

Be cheerful. Keep things in good repair. Keep your spirits up.
Think in harmony. Be agreeable. Do all that, and the God of love
and peace will be with you for sure.

2 Corinthians 13:11 MSG

Cheerfulness is a gift that we give to others and to ourselves. And, as believers who have been saved by a risen Christ, why shouldn't we be cheerful? The answer, of course, is that we have every reason to honor our Savior with joy in our hearts, smiles on our faces, and words of celebration on our lips.

Few things in life are more sad, or, for that matter, more absurd, than the sight of grumpy Christians trudging unhappily through life. Christ promises us lives of abundance and joy if we accept His love and His grace. Yet sometimes, even the most righteous among us are beset by fits of ill temper and frustration. During these moments, we may not feel like turning our thoughts and prayers to Christ, but that's precisely what we should do.

Mrs. Charles E. Cowman, the author of the classic devotional text *Streams in the Desert*, wrote, "Two wings are necessary to lift our souls toward God: prayer and praise. Prayer asks. Praise accepts the answer." That's why we should find the time to lift our concerns to God in prayer, and to praise Him for all that He has done.

John Wesley correctly observed, "Sour godliness is the devil's religion." These words remind us that pessimism and doubt are some of the most important tools that Satan uses to achieve his objectives. Our challenge, of course, is to ensure that Satan cannot use these tools on us.

Are you a cheerful Christian? You should be! And what is the best way to attain the joy that is rightfully yours? By giving Christ what is rightfully His: your heart, your soul, and your life.

When we bring sunshine into the lives of others, we're warmed by it ourselves. When we spill a little happiness, it splashes on us.

Barbara Johnson

Values for Life

Cheer up somebody else. Do you need a little cheering up? If so, find somebody else who needs cheering up, too. Then, do your best to brighten that person's day. When you do, you'll discover that cheering up other people is a wonderful way to cheer yourself up, too!

Timeless Wisdom for Godly Living

Christ can put a spring in your step and a thrill in your heart. Optimism and cheerfulness are products of knowing Christ.

Billy Graham

Be assured, my dear friend, that it is no joy to God in seeing you with a dreary countenance.

C. H. Spurgeon

Is anyone cheerful? He should sing praises.
James 5:13 HCSB

When I think of God, my heart is so full of joy that the notes leap and dance as they leave my pen; and since God has given me a cheerful heart, I serve him with a cheerful spirit.

Franz Joseph Haydn

Sour godliness is the devil's religion.

John Wesley

Be merry, really merry. The life of a true Christian should be a perpetual jubilee, a prelude to the festivals of eternity.

Theophare Venard

More Words from God's Word

Do everything readily and cheerfully—no bickering, no second-guessing allowed! Go out into the world uncorrupted, a breath of fresh air in this squalid and polluted society. Provide people with a glimpse of good living and of the living God. Carry the light-giving Message into the night.

Philippians 2:14-15 MSG

A cheerful heart brings a smile to your face; a sad heart makes it hard to get through the day.

Proverbs 15:13 MSG

Bright eyes cheer the heart; good news strengthens the bones.

Proverbs 15:30 HCSB

A cheerful disposition is good for your health; gloom and doom leave you bone-tired.

Proverbs 17:22 MSG

My Values for Life

I consider this day—and every day—to be a gift from God and a cause for celebration.

I do my best to maintain a positive attitude and a cheerful disposition, even when I'm tired or frustrated, or both.

I focus my thoughts on opportunities, not problems.

Check Your Value		
High	Med.	Low
—	—	—
—	—	—
—	—	—

Living above the Daily Whine

Therefore, since Christ suffered in his body, arm yourselves also with the same attitude, because he who has suffered in his body is done with sin. As a result, he does not live the rest of his earthly life for evil human desires, but rather for the will of God.

1 Peter 4:1-2 NIV

O f course you've heard the saying, "Life is what you make it." And although that statement may seem very trite, it's also very true. You can choose a life filled to the brim with frustration and fear, or you can choose a life of abundance and peace. That choice is up to you—and only you—and it depends, to a surprising extent, upon your attitude.

What's your attitude today? Are you fearful, angry, bored, or worried? Are you pessimistic, perplexed, pained, and perturbed? Are you moping around with a frown on your face that's almost as big as the one in your heart? If so, God wants to have a little talk with you.

God created you in His own image, and He wants you to experience joy, contentment, peace, and abundance. But, God will not force you to experience these things; you must claim them for yourself.

God has given you free will, including the ability to influence the direction and the tone of your thoughts. And, here's how God wants you to direct those thoughts:

Finally brothers, whatever is true, whatever is honorable, whatever is just, whatever is pure, whatever is lovely, whatever is commendable—if there is any moral excellence and if there is any praise—dwell on these things" (Philippians 4:8 HCSB).

The quality of your attitude will help determine the quality of your life, so you must guard your thoughts accordingly. If you make up your mind to approach life with a healthy mixture of realism and optimism, you'll be rewarded. But, if you allow yourself to fall into the unfortunate habit of negative thinking, you will doom yourself to unhappiness or mediocrity, or worse.

So, the next time you find yourself dwelling upon the negative aspects of your life, refocus your attention on things positive. The next time you find yourself falling prey to the blight of pessimism, stop yourself and turn your thoughts around. The next time you're tempted to waste valuable time gossiping or complaining, resist those temptations with all your might.

And remember: You'll never whine your way to the top . . . so don't waste your breath.

The last of the human freedoms is to choose one's attitude in any given set of circumstances.

Viktor Frankl

Values for Life

A happy heart every day: Remember: you can choose to have a good attitude or a not-so good attitude. And it's a choice you make every day.

Timeless Wisdom for Godly Living

Your attitude is more important than your aptitude.

Zig Ziglar

The Reference Point for the Christian is the Bible. All values, judgments, and attitudes must be gauged in relationship to this Reference Point.

Ruth Bell Graham

*Set your minds on what is above,
not on what is on the earth.*

Colossians 3:2 HCSB

Never use your problem as an excuse for bad attitudes or behavior.

Joyce Meyer

Often, attitude is the only difference between success and failure.

John Maxwell

If the attitude of servanthood is learned by attending to God as Lord, then serving others will develop as a very natural way of life.

Eugene Peterson

More Words from God's Word

For the word of God is living and active. Sharper than any double-edged sword, it penetrates even to dividing soul and spirit, joints and marrow; it judges the thoughts and attitudes of the heart.

Hebrews 4:12 NIV

Your attitude should be the same that Christ Jesus had.

Philippians 2:5 NLT

You were taught, with regard to your former way of life, to put off your old self, which is being corrupted by its deceitful desires; to be made new in the attitude of your minds; and to put on the new self, created to be like God in true righteousness and holiness.

Ephesians 4:22-24 NIV

My Values for Life

I believe that if I want to change certain aspects of my life, I also need to make adjustments in my own attitudes toward life.

I believe that it is important to associate myself with people who are upbeat, optimistic, and encouraging.

I believe that it is important to focus my thoughts on the positive aspects of life, not the negative ones.

Check Your Value		
High	Med.	Low
—	—	—
—	—	—
—	—	—

Attitude

The Righteous Life

For the Lord knows the way of the righteous,
but the way of the ungodly shall perish.

Psalm 1:6 NKJV

O swald Chambers, the author of the Christian classic devotional text *My Utmost for His Highest*, advised, "Never support an experience which does not have God as its source, and faith in God as its result." These words serve as a powerful reminder that, as Christians, we are called to walk with God and obey His commandments. But, we live in a world that presents us with countless temptations to stray far from God's path. We Christians, when confronted with sin, have clear instructions: Walk—or better yet run—in the opposite direction.

When we seek righteousness in our own lives—and when we seek the companionship of those who do likewise—we reap the spiritual rewards that God intends for our lives. When we behave ourselves as godly men and women, we honor God. When we live righteously and according to God's commandments, He blesses us in ways that we cannot fully understand.

Each new day presents countless opportunities to put God in first place . . . or not. When we honor Him by living according to His commandments, we earn for ourselves the abundance and peace that He promises. But, when we concern ourselves more with pleasing others than with pleasing our Creator, we bring needless suffering upon ourselves and our families. Would you like a time-tested formula for successful living? Here is a formula that is proven and true: Seek God's approval in every aspect of your life. Does this sound too simple? Perhaps it is simple, but it is also the only way to reap the marvelous riches that God has in store for you.

So today, take every step of your journey with God as your traveling companion. Read His Word and follow His commandments. Support only those activities that further God's kingdom and your spiritual growth. Be an example of righteous living to your friends, to your neighbors, and to your children. Then, reap the blessings that God has promised to all those who live according to His will and His Word.

Righteousness not only defines God,
but God defines righteousness.

Bill Hybels

Values for Life

Righteous living is not just for some special few but for everyone. Elisabeth Elliot writes: " Let us never suppose that obedience is impossible or that holiness is meant only for a select few. Our Shepherd leads us in paths of righteousness—not for our name's sake but for His."

Timeless Wisdom for Godly Living

If we don't hunger and thirst after righteousness, we'll become anemic and feel miserable in our Christian experience.

Franklin Graham

Our souls were made to live in an upper atmosphere, and we stifle and choke if we live on any lower level. Our eyes were made to look off from these heavenly heights, and our vision is distorted by any lower gazing.

Hannah Whitall Smith

But by His doing you are in Christ Jesus, who became to us wisdom from God, and righteousness and sanctification, and redemption.

1 Corinthians 1:30 NASB

Holiness is not God's asking us to be "good"; it is an invitation to be "His."

Lisa Bevere

Sanctify yourself and you will sanctify society.

St. Francis of Assisi

Simplicity reaches out after God; purity discovers and enjoys him.

Thomas à Kempis

More Words from God's Word

But now you must be holy in everything you do, just as God—who chose you to be his children—is holy. For he himself has said, "You must be holy because I am holy."

1 Peter 1:15-16 NLT

For the eyes of the Lord are on the righteous, and His ears are open to their prayers; but the face of the Lord is against those who do evil.

1 Peter 3:12 NKJV

Walk in a manner worthy of the God who calls you into His own kingdom and glory.

1 Thessalonians 2:12 NASB

Discipline yourself for the purpose of godliness.

1 Timothy 4:7 NASB

My Values for Life

I understand the value of living a life that is pleasing to God.

As my own example for living, I look to Jesus.

I understand the importance of setting a good example for my family and friends.

Check Your Value		
High	Med.	Low
—	—	—
—	—	—
—	—	—

Tackling Tough Times

We also rejoice in our sufferings, because we know that suffering produces perseverance; perseverance, character; and character, hope.

Romans 5:3-4 NIV

As life here on earth unfolds, all of us encounter occasional disappointments and setbacks: Those occasional visits from Old Man Trouble are simply a fact of life, and none of us are exempt. When tough times arrive, we may be forced to rearrange our plans and our priorities. But even on our darkest days, we must remember that God's love remains constant.

The fact that we encounter adversity is not nearly so important as the way we choose to deal with it. When tough times arrive, we have a clear choice: we can begin the difficult work of tackling our troubles . . . or not. When we summon the courage to look Old Man Trouble squarely in the eye, he usually blinks. But, if we refuse to address our problems, even the smallest annoyances have a way of growing into king-sized catastrophes.

Psalm 145 promises, "The Lord is near to all who call on him, to all who call on him in truth. He fulfills the desires of those who fear him; he hears their cry and saves them" (vv. 18-20 NIV). And the words of Jesus offer us comfort: "These things I have spoken to you, that in Me you may have peace. In the world you will have

tribulation; but be of good cheer, I have overcome the world"
(John 16:33 NKJV).

As believers, we know that God loves us and that He will
protect us. In times of hardship, He will comfort us; in times of
sorrow, He will dry our tears. When we are troubled or weak or
sorrowful, God is always with us. We must build our lives on the
rock that cannot be shaken: we must trust in God. And then, we
must get on with the hard work of tackling our problems . . . because
if we don't, who will? Or should?

When you feel that all is lost,
sometimes the greatest gain is ready
to be yours.

Thomas à Kempis

Values for Life

Tough Times Help Us Grow: If you're going through difficult times,
consider it an opportunity for spiritual growth. Elisabeth Elliot
correctly observes, "God's curriculum will always include lessons we
wish we could skip. With an intimate understanding of our deepest
needs and individual capacities, He chooses our curriculum." So ask
yourself this question: "What is God trying to teach me today?"

Timeless Wisdom for Godly Living

When problems threaten to engulf us, we must do what believers have always done, turn to the Lord for encouragement and solace. As Psalm 46:1 states, "God is our refuge and strength, an ever-present help in trouble."

Shirley Dobson

God helps those who help themselves, but there are times when we are quite incapable of helping ourselves. That's when God stoops down and gathers us in His arms like a mother lifts a sick child, and does for us what we cannot do for ourselves.

Ruth Bell Graham

The Lord is a shelter for the oppressed, a refuge in times of trouble. Those who know your name trust in you, for you, O LORD, have never abandoned anyone who searches for you.

Psalm 9:10 NLT

Your greatest ministry will likely come out of your greatest hurt.

Rick Warren

God will not permit any troubles to come upon us unless He has a specific plan by which great blessing can come out of the difficulty.

Peter Marshall

More Words from God's Word

Cast your burden on the Lord, and He will support you; He will never allow the righteous to be shaken.

Psalm 55:22 HCSB

Don't fret or worry. Instead of worrying, pray. Let petitions and praises shape your worries into prayers, letting God know your concerns. Before you know it, a sense of God's wholeness, everything coming together for good, will come and settle you down. It's wonderful what happens when Christ displaces worry at the center of your life.

Philippians 4:6-7 MSG

Come to Me, all you who labor and are heavy laden, and I will give you rest. Take My yoke upon you and learn from Me, for I am gentle and lowly in heart, and you will find rest for your souls. For My yoke is easy and My burden is light.

Matthew 11:28-30 NKJV

My Values for Life

In dealing with difficult situations, I view God as my comfort and my strength.

I believe that difficult times can also be times of intense personal growth.

I understand the importance of comforting others who find themselves in difficult circumstances.

Check Your Value		
High	Med.	Low
—	—	—
—	—	—
—	—	—

Acceptance for Today

He is the Lord. Let him do what he thinks is best.

1 Samuel 3:18 NCV

The American theologian Reinhold Niebuhr composed a profoundly simple verse that came to be known as the Serenity Prayer: "God, grant me the serenity to accept the things I cannot change, the courage to change the things I can, and the wisdom to know the difference." Niebuhr's words are far easier to recite than they are to live by. Why? Because most of us want life to unfold in accordance with our own wishes and timetables. But sometimes God has other plans.

Author Hannah Whitall Smith observed, "How changed our lives would be if we could only fly through the days on wings of surrender and trust!" These words remind us that even when we cannot understand the workings of God, we must trust Him and accept His will.

So if you've encountered unfortunate circumstances that are beyond your power to control, accept those circumstances . . . and trust God. When you do, you can be comforted in the knowledge that your Creator is both loving and wise, and that He understands His plans perfectly, even when you do not.

Acceptance says: True, this is my situation at the moment. I'll look unblinkingly at the reality of it. But, I'll also open my hands to accept willingly whatever a loving father sends me.

Catherine Marshall

The more comfortable we are with mystery in our journey, the more rest we will know along the way.

John Eldredge

Values for Life

You should learn from the past, but you should never allow yourself to become stuck there. Once you have made peace with the past, you are free to live more fully in the present . . . and that's precisely what you should do.

Timeless Wisdom for Godly Living

Acceptance is resting in God's goodness, believing that He has all things under His control.

Charles Swindoll

Loving Him means the thankful acceptance of all things that His love has appointed.

Elisabeth Elliot

> *For everything created by God is good, and nothing should be rejected if it is received with thanksgiving.*
> 1 Timothy 4:4 HCSB

How changed our lives would be if we could only fly through the days on wings of surrender and trust!

Hannah Whitall Smith

The will of God for your life is simply that you submit yourself to Him each day and say, "Father, Your will for today is mine. Your pleasure for today is mine. Your work for today is mine. I trust You to be God. You lead me today and I will follow."

Kay Arthur

More Words from God's Word

He said, "I came naked from my mother's womb, and I will be stripped of everything when I die. The LORD gave me everything I had, and the LORD has taken it away. Praise the name of the LORD!"

Job 1:21 NLT

Should we accept only good things from the hand of God and never anything bad?

Job 2:10 NLT

Come to terms with God and be at peace; in this way good will come to you.

Job 22:21 HCSB

Do you think for a minute I'm not going to drink this cup the Father gave me?

John 18:11 MSG

My Values for Life

I believe that it is important to trust God even when I don't understand why certain things happen.

I think it is important to learn from the past, to accept the past, and to live in the present.

I think it is important to change what I need to change and accept that which I can't change.

Check Your Value		
High	Med.	Low
—	—	—
—	—	—
—	—	—

This Is the Day...

This is the day which the LORD has made;
let us rejoice and be glad in it.

Psalm 118:24 NASB

The familiar words of Psalm 118 remind us that today, like every day, is a priceless gift from God. What do you expect from the day ahead? Are you expecting God to do wonderful things, or are you living beneath a cloud of apprehension and doubt? Do you expect God to use you in unexpected ways, or do you expect another uneventful day to pass with little fanfare? As a thoughtful believer, the answer to these questions should be obvious.

C. H. Spurgeon, the renowned 19th-century English clergyman, advised, "Rejoicing is clearly a spiritual command. To ignore it, I need to remind you, is disobedience." As Christians, we are called by our Creator to live abundantly, prayerfully, and joyfully. To do otherwise is to squander His spiritual gifts.

Christ came to this earth to give us abundant life and eternal salvation. Our task is to accept Christ's grace with joy in our hearts and praise on our lips. When we fashion our days around Jesus, we are transformed: we see the world differently, we act differently, and we feel differently about ourselves and our neighbors.

If you're a thoughtful Christian, then you're a thankful

Christian. And because of your faith, you can face the inevitable challenges and disappointments of each day armed with the joy of Christ and the promise of salvation.

So whatever this day holds for you, begin it and end it with God as your partner and Christ as your Savior. And throughout the day, give thanks to the One who created you and saved you. God's love for you is infinite—accept it joyfully and be thankful.

Wherever you are, be all there.
Live to the hilt every situation
you believe to be the will of God.

Jim Elliot

Values for Life

Today's Journey: Life is a journey, and today is an important part of that journey. Yet we may be tempted to take this day—along with the ones that precede it and the ones that follow it—for granted. When we do, Satan rejoices. Today, like every other day, provides countless opportunities to serve God and to worship Him. But, if we turn our backs on our Creator, or if we simply become too busy to acknowledge His greatness, we do a profound disservice to ourselves, to our families, and to our world.

Timeless Wisdom for Godly Living

Men spend their lives in anticipation, in determining to be vastly happy at some period or other, when they have time. But the present time has one advantage over every other: it is ours.

Charles Caleb Colton

> *You must choose for yourselves today whom you will serve . . . as for me and my family, we will serve the Lord.*
>
> *Joshua 24:15 NCV*

A glimpse of the next three feet of road is more important and useful than a view of the horizon.

C. S. Lewis

It has been well said that no man ever sank under the burden of the day. It is when tomorrow's burden is added to the burden of today that the weight is more than a man can bear. Never load yourselves so, my friends. If you find yourselves so loaded, at least remember this: it is your own doing, not God's. He begs you to leave the future to Him and mind the present.

George MacDonald

Each day, each moment is so pregnant with eternity that if we "tune in" to it, we can hardly contain the joy.

Gloria Gaither

More Words from God's Word

While it is daytime, we must continue doing the work of the One who sent me. Night is coming, when no one can work.

John 9:4 NCV

Give your entire attention to what God is doing right now, and don't get worked up about what may or may not happen tomorrow. God will help you deal with whatever hard things come up when the time comes.

Matthew 6:34 MSG

When you and your children return to the LORD your God and obey him with all your heart and with all your soul according to everything I command you today, then the LORD your God will restore your fortunes and have compassion on you and gather you again from all the nations where he scattered you.

Deuteronomy 30:2-3 NIV

My Values for Life

I understand that today is a precious gift.

I trust that the way I choose to live today will have a profound impact on my future.

I believe that it is important to live passionately, obediently, and joyfully.

Check Your Value		
High	Med.	Low
—	—	—
—	—	—
—	—	—

Index of Topics

Acceptance   308

Adversity   304

Anger   252

Attitude   296

Behavior   94

Character   82

Cheerfulness   292

Comforting Others   280

Communication   284

Conscience   272

Contentment   268

Courage   260

Dating   256

Devotional   70

Difficult Days   248

Disappointment and Failure   210

Dreams   146

Encouragement   244

Faith   236

Family   232

Fitness   178

Following Christ   224

Forgiveness   220

Friends	288
Giving	216
God's Grace	206
God's Guidance	158
God's Love	202
God's Plans	190
God's Power	240
God's Presence	194
God's Timing	118
Golden Rule	182
Helping Others	174
Hope	166
Humility	46
Joy	162
Knowledge	228
Life	154
Loneliness	150
Love	142
Materialism	58
Obedience	138
Opportunities	134
Optimism	126
Patience	276
Peace	122
Peer Pressure	130
Perfectionism	114

Perspective 110

Possessions 102

Procrastination 98

Purpose 34

Questions 90

Renewal 86

Righteousness 300

Self-esteem 78

Service 198

Simplicity 186

Speech 106

Spiritual Growth 74

Talents 264

Testimony 66

Thanksgiving 62

The Bible 170

Thoughts 54

Time 50

Today 312

Transformation 42

Truth 38

Values 14

Wisdom 22

Work 30

Worry 26

Worship 18